LIBERTARIANISM
FOR BEGINNERS®

Praise for

Libertarianism For Beginners

Todd Seavey has written one of *the* best introductions to libertarianism ever. It's clear, concise, compelling—and fun!

Donald Boudreaux, economist at George Mason University and the Mercatus Center, blogger at Café Hayek

Many a curious liberal, conservative, or apolitical moderate has walked away from a conversation with a libertarian more confused than edified. They need this book.

Libertarianism confuses non-libertarians—because it's different in kind from other political philosophies, and because libertarians themselves spend so much breath on internecine warfare. Author Todd Seavey and cartoonist Nathan Smith have just the solution to that problem: a clear, concise exposition of libertarian thought that elucidates without proselytizing. They acknowledge and explain the internal rifts of libertarianism, without taking sides or getting sucked down rabbit holes.

If you want to understand libertarianism (and you should) start with this book.

Tim Carney, *Washington Examiner* senior political columnist and author of *The Big Ripoff*

Seavey provides a sober and sane introduction to, and defense of, a wild and radical philosophy whose relevance to the world, and popularity, gets more and more apparent by the year. Reducing a complicated body of thought in ways that are clearly understandable but never misleadingly simple, assessing both a body of thought and the often flawed humans who kept it alive, up to date on the tangled internal politics of the movement and timeless in showing how keeping your eye on the libertarian conception of property rights should guide your understanding of what libertarians think and why.

Brian Doherty, *Reason* magazine senior editor and author of *Radicals for Capitalism*

Libertarianism can be a difficult philosophy to understand—heck, most libertarians don't even know what it actually is. From the basic concept of free will to abstract ones like the non-aggression principle, *Libertarianism for Beginners* provides a comprehensive guide to what drives the movement. And with such wit and clarity, it should serve as a guide for all—neophytes or neocons—on how to talk to and/or understand the libertarian in your life.

Andrew Kirell, *Daily Beast* senior editor

Libertarianism has gotten a bad name from all the gun nuts, crackpots and trailer-park hermits that have besmirched a noble tradition of proudly American anti-authoritarianism. As such, there is no one in the world whom I want to explain libertarianism to me more than the always exciting, always exhilarating, and never indulgent Todd Seavey, a thinking man's Plato.

Gersh Kuntzman, *New York Daily News* reporter

Seavey provides a thorough and easy to read explanation of libertarianism and its history. Full of examples and nuance, the book offers a balanced context for understanding this philosophy.

Ann Lee, NYU Stern School of Business professor and author of *What the U.S. Can Learn from China*

The briefest introduction to libertarianism is also one of the richest—Seavey brilliantly captures a many-sided movement.

Daniel McCarthy, editor of *American Conservative* magazine

Libertarian is a word too often used as a cheap punch-line or a put-down by those unwilling, or perhaps afraid, to understand what it really means. In this fantastic book—one both learned and lighthearted—Todd Seavey rescues libertarianism from the finger-pointers and makes a lucid, convincing case for its relevance as a serious and necessary political philosophy. *Everyone,* not just "beginners," will benefit from reading it. I most certainly did—and I'm not even a libertarian.

Alexander Rose, author of *Washington's Spies*

If you've ever suspected your political views could boil down to something as simple as "leave me alone, and I'll leave you alone," Todd Seavey's wonderfully clarifying book is a must for you. In level-headed, precise, simple, and jargon-free language, Seavey lays out how rejecting the impulse to control others' bodies and property can be the basis of a coherent system of thinking towards a more rational and happier society.

Kyle Smith, *New York Post* columnist

America may or not be living through its latest libertarian moment but Americans—and not just Americans—will have a much clearer understanding of what this might mean if they read Todd Seavey's *Libertarianism for Beginners*, a brisk, smart, and sympathetic field guide to libertarianism, its tribes, its thinkers, and ten, not commandments of course, but dilemmas. Feel free to buy this book.

Andrew Stuttaford, *National Review* contributing editor

This is a wonderfully crisp and elegant introduction to libertarianism—and it's so smart that it's not just for beginners. It's a concise, evenhanded guide to one of the most influential intellectual movements today. No matter what your ideology, this masterful survey of history and philosophy will give you a new perspective on politics and government—and keep you entertained while you learn.

John Tierney, columnist and co-author of *Willpower: Rediscovering the Greatest Human Strength*

LIBERTARIANISM
FOR BEGINNERS®

BY TODD SEAVEY • ILLUSTRATIONS BY NATHAN SMITH

Foreword by John Stossel

FOR BEGINNERS®

For Beginners LLC
155 Main Street, Suite 211
Danbury, CT 06810 USA
www.forbeginnersbooks.com

Text: © 2016 Todd Seavey
Illustrations: © 2016 Nathan Smith

A For Beginners® Documentary Comic Book
Copyright © 2016

Cataloging-in-Publication information is available from the Library of Congress.

ISBN-13: 978-1-939994-66-0

Manufactured in the United States of America

For Beginners® and Beginners Documentary Comic Books® are published
by For Beginners LLC.

First Edition

10 9 8 7 6 5 4 3 2 1

CONTENTS

FOREWORD

by John Stossel

Teaching people libertarian ideas is tough. I try to do it on television, in books, and in videos for high school teachers. I worry sometimes about whether it gets through.

I have mostly worked for news organizations, so that means looking for recent events that illustrate larger points. Just as there are trade-offs at the heart of economics, there are trade-offs in picking which stories to tell.

Television needs to be, well, visual. Television requires energy and good talkers and catchy examples people may talk about the next day. It's easier to put those pieces together when the topic is something concrete and easy to understand—like the disasters, crimes, and wars that dominate news coverage. When the topic is something abstract, like laws of supply and demand or the tendency of constitutional freedoms to erode in times of crisis, it gets tougher.

Critics accuse me of oversimplifying. Of course I oversimplify; I work in television. Someone who wants deeper knowledge should read the original sources—books by libertarian economists like Milton Friedman and Friedrich Hayek. But most won't.

So read the book you hold in your hands. It falls somewhere in between the simplicity of TV and the thoroughness of Ludwig von Mises' *Human Action*. It's written by my sometime libertarian colleague Todd Seavey, with cartoons by Nathan Smith. Todd seemed obsessed with comic books back when he worked for me at ABC News, so I shouldn't be surprised he's collaborating with a cartoonist.

Libertarianism For Beginners is one more attempt to explain important philosophical ideas that, for some reason, the world hasn't latched onto yet. It gives you some of the history of those ideas and the economic and philosophical arguments in favor of them.

It may not persuade you to become a libertarian, but its purpose is to help you understand where we libertarians come from. That's useful in a culture where libertarian voices are often drowned out by conventional conservatives and liberals. Some of them call us libertarians crazy.

But as this book points out, the libertarian philosophy is not completely detached from other political traditions. *Libertarianism For Beginners* traces connections between libertarianism and the older philosophies of liberalism and conservatism. Seavey thinks he understands where those older philosophies went wrong and where liberty might solve problems that the pro-government philosophies created. I think he's onto something.

These arguments will never end. But this is a good place to begin understanding them.

Award-winning television journalist and political commentator John Stossel is the host of "Stossel," a weekly program on the Fox Business Network with a libertarian viewpoint. He also appears regularly as a guest analyst on various Fox News programs. In the past he co-anchored ABC's primetime newsmagazine show "20/20," served as consumer editor for "Good Morning America," and reported for WCBS-TV in New York City. He is also the author of three books, numerous magazine articles and newspaper columns, and multimedia materials for use in schools.

INTRODUCTION

Nearly all political philosophies present some vision of the good life or political power and ask how to impose that vision on the general populace.

One philosophy, growing in popularity in the twenty-first century, instead seeks to prevent people from imposing their political visions on each other. Libertarianism asks not "Who will run the government?" but instead poses questions such as "Do we really need a government?" and "Isn't your life your own?"

> "PEOPLE HAVE DIFFERENT CONCEPTS OF THE GOOD LIFE, AND ANY ATTEMPT TO IMPOSE ONE FAVORED VIEW WILL BE CONTENTIOUS."
>
> **PHILOSOPHER LOREN LOMASKY**
> IN *REASON* MAGAZINE

The details of libertarian philosophy remain a mystery to most people and a source of controversy even among those more familiar with these ideas. Government itself, by contrast, gets low approval ratings from the general public yet is widely assumed to be a *necessary* evil.

What if we conclude that government is both evil and unnecessary (or largely unnecessary)? To better understand how some people in our society have arrived at that radical conclusion, let's take a closer look at libertarianism. It comes in many forms, from conservative-leaning "paleolibertarians" to capitalism-wary "left-libertarians," with Ayn Rand fans, moderately pro-welfare "liberaltarians," and just-plain free-market-loving mainstream libertarians somewhere in between.

But first . . .

THE BASICS

ESTIMATES VARY, BUT WHEN THE
libertarian Cato Institute did an opinion survey
designed to find out if Americans were both **"SOCIALLY
LIBERAL"** (not wanting the government to interfere in
their personal behavior) and **"FISCALLY CONSER-
VATIVE"** (wanting low taxes, low government spending,
and few regulations), they found that 15%–19% of the population may thus qualify as libertarians (loosely defined).
The number who actually think of themselves as libertarians is much smaller, perhaps 5% or less of the population.
The Libertarian Party, which wins only about one quar-
ter or one third of self-proclaimed libertarians' votes in
presidential elections, struggles to win more than 1% of
the general electorate.

Ultimately, however, libertarianism isn't about winning elections. It doesn't even promise to win over the
rest of society to its views, though libertarians will sometimes try. It is first and foremost a political *philosophy*—
a description of how, in the opinion of libertarians, free

people ought to treat one another, at least in the use of the law, which they regard as potentially dangerous. If libertarians are correct, **THE LAW SHOULD INTRUDE INTO PEOPLE'S LIVES AS LITTLE AS POSSIBLE**, rarely telling them what to do or how to live.

That sounds pleasant and easy-going enough—live and let live! So why are libertarians so often despised and ridiculed? As is often the case with an unfamiliar philosophy, many people are prepared to believe the worst about libertarianism and, understandably, may not be motivated to seek out the best and brightest champions of the philosophy.

Hearing only cursory descriptions from critics of libertarianism—on both the left and the right—the casual observer might be left with the impression that libertarians, because they are laissez-faire capitalists, recommend that we stop caring about the poor (or even that we hate the poor) and that we allow commercial enterprises to sell poisonous food or exploding vehicles without legal consequences, all the while permitting greedy millionaires to buy up forests and burn them down for no reason.

As you may have guessed, this is not a very accurate picture. And since libertarianism has been getting a *little* more popular lately, you may be relieved to hear that.

LIBERTARIANISM IS A POLITICAL PHILOSO-PHY THAT EMPHASIZES INDIVIDUAL RIGHTS, including strong property rights, and the radical shrinking or abolition of government (since government routinely interferes with your use of your body and property). Libertarians believe, roughly stated, that *you have the right to do as you please with your own body and your own possessions so long as you do not use the body or possessions of others without their permission.*

I WILL NOT BE PUSHED, FILED, STAMPED, INDEXED, BRIEFED, DEBRIEFED, OR NUMBERED! MY LIFE IS MY OWN!

LINE FROM THE TV SERIES
THE PRISONER

The principle of "like liberty" for everyone has been articulated, in varying forms, by the likes of nineteenth-century British philosopher John Stuart Mill, whom we'll hear more about later. As it is sometimes summarized, Mill's view was that your right to swing your fist ends at the tip of his nose. Do what you like, but don't harm others.

Even Mill was arguably not a full-fledged libertarian, though, and this book is partly about how the contemporary philosophy with that name arose gradually from its intellectual forebears over the course of several centuries.

DEFINING TERMS

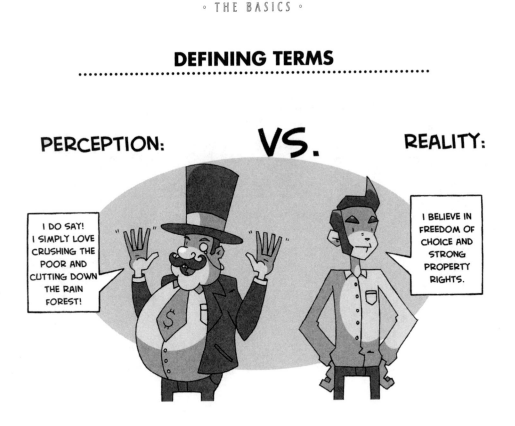

The meaning of the word "libertarianism" may have been fought over even more frequently than libertarian policy proposals themselves.

In twenty-first-century U.S. political parlance, and for most purposes in this book, the word refers broadly to *a political philosophy that advocates the shrinking (or even elimination) of government; preserving the freedom of individuals to control their own lives; and making strong property rights a central feature of law and a bulwark against interference by the state in personal decision-making.*

Beyond these basic principles, however, there is often furious disagreement over how to define "libertarian." Indeed, as in so many disputes in public life, fighting over terminology becomes a means of fighting over boundaries with tribal fierceness. There is a temptation to think that if one cannot quite defeat an opposing argument, one can at least excommunicate the person making the argument on the basis of terminology, minimizing the chance of the contagion spreading to the rest of the movement.

This book will not use any artfully designed or overly restrictive definitions of "libertarian" in an effort to dismiss or conceal troublesome or divisive arguments. It will be assumed throughout that there are *always* more caveats and clarifications that could be provided. The goal here is to explain, not exclude. This will be a basic, consensus view of what libertarianism is, and areas of disagreement among libertarians will be noted as impartially as possible. This does not mean that there are no correct answers when disagreements arise, only that this book is an attempt to describe what an array of views and subsidiary movements *have in common* rather than to describe one narrow version of those views.

All philosophical movements, whether political, religious, social, or economic, have internal disagreements. But disagreement is not necessarily the same as logical contradiction. Differences of emphasis are not necessarily insurmountable rifts, nor evidence that someone on one side or the other is engaged in deceit. Widely differing premises may lead people of good will to very similar conclusions. Similar premises may also lead people of good will to divergent conclusions, with all of them still in one movement, or in closely associated movements, working together on most issues.

Beyond libertarianism as defined above, however, the term has been used for other purposes by additional groups large enough that they should be acknowledged at the outset.

This is not to say that these other groups have no useful arguments or that they have no right to use the term.

(Most students of political philosophy wish there were more precise labels for the dizzying array of ideas and factions in the world.) Libertarians have no desire to "steal" the term from anyone else; they are just using the current lexicon. These other groups, while interesting in their own right, are simply not the focus of this book.

Some of these rival meanings of the term—the kinds of "libertarianism" this book does *not* explain—are as follows:

5 THINGS THIS BOOK IS NOT ABOUT

1 Beginning in the eighteenth century, the term "libertarian" was sometimes used to connote belief in the existence of **"free will"** in the sense that philosophers mean it—that is, the opposite of "determinism," which is the control of all human decision-making by causal factors such as climate, biology, and historical circumstance.

Around the same time, the term "liberal" (itself open to many interpretations) came to mean politically anti-authoritarian and characterized by respect for individual autonomy. "Libertarian" in our sense means something *similar* but hardly identical to what "liberal" meant to people of the eighteenth and nineteenth century, as will be explained later.

2 The term "libertarian" (or an approximation of the word in other languages) is sometimes used in Continental Europe and associated regions to denote a philosophy closer to **Marxism** or **socialism** in orientation — that is, anti-property rather than pro-property.

Association (or confusion) with our definition of libertarianism lies in the fact that Continental European users of the term often see themselves as "liberating" people from economic or historical circumstances. It bears emphasizing that their policy recommendations are nearly the opposite of the ones contemporary American libertarians urge. The two strains interact and influence each other very little. (Yanis Varoufakis, the Greek finance minister who resigned during that nation's debt crisis of 2015, called himself a "libertarian Marxist.")

3 Bearing greater affinity with libertarians as we define them are American anarchists, who sometimes use the term "libertarian" as a near synonym of **"anarchist"** (yet another term with multiple meanings). But anarchism is often

taken to imply opposition to *both* government and capitalism (and other organized systems). Linguist and leftist political commentator Noam Chomsky has sometimes used the term in that sense. The brand of libertarians examined in this book, by contrast, generally opposes government but supports capitalism (though even that term has been used in conflicting ways and was coined as a slur by the consummate *anti*-capitalist, Karl Marx).

4 "Libertarian" is sometimes used, especially in the United States, as a shortened form of **"civil libertarian."** The latter term, however, connotes a somewhat vaguer philosophy that is often, but not always, compatible with our libertarianism. That set of principles animates the American Civil Liberties Union, for example, which tends to place a greater emphasis on specific constitutional, legal, or procedural rights (or purported rights) that may or may not be compatible with property rights. Civil libertarians at times override property rights completely and call for substantial intervention on the part of the government. Libertarians

in our sense of the word will often, but not always, agree with civil libertarians.

5 Further complicating the lexicon, there are people who are quite familiar with the meaning of "libertarian" as used in this book but who use it to describe **only certain aspects** of their own (or others') views rather than a coherent, consistent philosophy. That is, people sometimes claim to be "a libertarian on fiscal issues" or "a libertarian about drugs" without being in favor of more sweeping deregulation of human activity. Sometimes people casually self-identify as "libertarian" *without* extending libertarian arguments to all aspects of life, often to the confusion of the general public.

Hardcore libertarians sometimes debate whether it is helpful to have such people engage in public discourse or whether it is counterproductive as a source of confusion, if not deliberate obfuscation. Regardless, we are primarily concerned in this book with the philosophical arguments in favor of being "libertarian about everything," so to speak.

OTHER COMMON TERMS IN THE LIBERTARIAN LEXICON

SO WHAT IS PROPERTY ANYWAY?

Though not all full-fledged libertarians treat **property rights** as the foundation of their political philosophy—and even the most ardent advocates of strong property rights normally have deeper reasons for advocating them—thinking about property does provide a convenient framework for predicting what moral and political positions libertarians will take.

In referring to "property rights," libertarians do *not* mean whatever property claims happen to be enforceable under the current legal system. They mean the rights that *ought* to be enforced regarding property in a fully (or nearly) libertarian society. Thus, if a libertarian says she favors strict enforcement of property rights, it does not mean that she endorses, say, a legal claim the government has granted you to your neighbor's house under eminent domain laws that might allow you to build a Walmart or highway off-ramp on his property. Likewise, since libertarians assume that individuals own their own bodies, it does not mean that slave owners have any legitimate claim to slaves.

According to libertarians, your body, like all your property, should be yours to do with as you please so long as you do not harm the body or property of others without their permission. Your property rights exist as moral claims even if society fails to recognize them—indeed, even if society actively undermines them or passes laws that make it difficult for you to exercise them.

The violation of property rights, then, is nearly always seen by libertarians as an authoritarian intrusion, both morally and legally illegitimate. Such violations are regarded as **coercion**, in the special libertarian sense of the term. Different factions of libertarians (all within the main sense of the word as used in this book) may disagree as to whether coercion should be completely eliminated, minimized, or merely limited to certain narrow forms.

Nevertheless, most libertarians understand the basic sense in which the word "coercion" is used here (even if they don't routinely invoke the term).

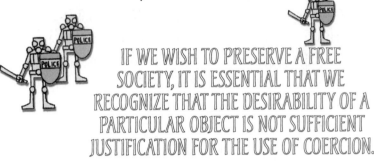

IF WE WISH TO PRESERVE A FREE SOCIETY, IT IS ESSENTIAL THAT WE RECOGNIZE THAT THE DESIRABILITY OF A PARTICULAR OBJECT IS NOT SUFFICIENT JUSTIFICATION FOR THE USE OF COERCION.

FRIEDRICH HAYEK, *THE CONSTITUTION OF LIBERTY*

Coercion, then, in libertarian parlance, is roughly synonymous with property rights violations, including attacks on the body. Resistance to such violations lies at the core of libertarian philosophy. Retaliation or restitution for property rights violations—such as using a gun to repel a gun-wielding attacker—is not normally referred to as coercion by libertarians but rather as self-defense.

Thus, it is the ***initiation of force***, rather than its retaliatory use (or its restitution-seeking use), that libertarianism expressly forbids. Keep in mind that libertarians regard the taking of property without permission as the initiation of force as well. For instance, holding a gun on someone to prevent him from fraudulently removing a piece of your property might well be justified. *He* would be the initiator of force, not you, even though you are holding a gun and he might merely be holding a TV set he had removed from your house without your permission or under the false pretense of being a repairman.

Just as libertarians respect the right of individuals to control their bodies and other property, so they respect the right to retaliate against ***force and fraud***. Note that some libertarians might choose to be pacifists and never retaliate with more than a sternly worded letter, and most would prefer to outsource the job of retaliation to professional police or security guards. But libertarianism is gen-

erally taken to imply that victims are within their rights to retaliate with the force necessary to restore their property or defend their bodies.

When libertarians condemn **government** or **the state**, they refer specifically to the institution that most often and most routinely uses people's bodies and other property without permission, chiefly by regulating, taxing, or fining them. Libertarians do not deny the usefulness of rules reached by voluntary or contractual arrangement between individuals and that bind *only* those individuals. But they do not normally refer to such arrangements as "government." (Nor in this context do they mean "state" as in "state rather than federal," a frequent source of confusion in the context of U.S. law.)

It would be wrong, therefore, to accuse libertarians of being hypocrites who love government just because, say, they respect the right of individuals to form a bird-watching society or even a strict religious order. As long as individuals freely contract (whether in print or orally) to enter into such arrangements, they are still exercising control over their own bodies and property. And they are doing so even if they make a contract that gives the head of the religious order the right to rap them hard on the shoulders for falling asleep during religious gatherings (as is the custom in some Buddhist temples). But the moment the group begins to use the bodies or property of outsiders who never contracted to be in the group, as a government does, it is said to engage in coercion.

For libertarians, any large, centralized, coercive organization, especially one that claims a legal monopoly on the right to use force in a certain geographic area, is regarded as a government.

THE MOST DANGEROUS MAN TO ANY GOVERNMENT IS THE MAN WHO IS ABLE TO THINK THINGS OUT FOR HIMSELF, WITHOUT REGARD TO THE PREVAILING SUPERSTITIONS AND TABOOS. ALMOST INEVITABLY HE COMES TO THE CONCLUSION THAT THE GOVERNMENT HE LIVES UNDER IS DISHONEST, INSANE, AND INTOLERABLE, AND SO, IF HE IS ROMANTIC, HE TRIES TO CHANGE IT.

H.L. MENCKEN, IN THE MAGAZINE *THE SMART SET*

Other, less centralized forms of coercion certainly exist—such as terrorism, organized crime, gang crime, rape, slavery, burglary, kidnapping, and more—and libertarians morally reject all of these decentralized forms as well. (Critics of libertarianism often make the mistake of thinking that because libertarians spend so much time talking about government policy they are indifferent to other forms of coercion. Some critics even insist that libertarians logically ought to be indifferent to these other forms, thinking *only* government can stop them.)

Most libertarians, rightly or wrongly, complicate the legal and ethical picture by endorsing **limited government** rather than advocating no government at all. Libertarians who insist there should be none at all are called *anarcho-capitalists*. (How anarcho-

capitalists would solve basic problems of social coordi-
nation normally handled by the state will be discussed in
Chapter 7.) Libertarians who call for limited government
are sometimes referred to as *minarchists*—that is, advocates of a minimal state rather than no state.

But the term "limited government" does not immediately tell us what the precise limits on government action
should be. Indeed, libertarians disagree somewhat as to
how to draw the lines. One common way of distinguishing
between "legitimate" and "illegitimate" government action
is to make a distinction between (1) government actions
that merely enforce property rights and fund the minimal
systems necessary to protect them—chiefly, a court system, the police, and a purely defensive military; and (2)
government actions that go beyond that to impose other
restrictions or demands on what citizens can do with their
bodies and property, such as censorship, mandatory health
regimens, aesthetic building codes, laws against running
certain types of businesses, and taxes to fund an endless
variety of government spending.

In other words, the law should be defensive but not
offensive, protecting rights rather than violating them. In
the libertarian mind, the closer government gets to the
ideal of the ***"minimal state,"*** also referred to as the
"night watchman state," the better.

In libertarian parlance, someone who advocates more
pervasive government is called a **statist**, or an advocate
of statism. (Whether minarchism itself should be considered a form of statism, as some anarcho-capitalists allege,

may be a question of semantics, which we will revisit in Chapter 7.)

Human behavior that accords with the non-coercive ideal sketched in the preceding paragraphs, as well as the exchange of goods that occurs within those parameters, tend to be viewed by libertarians as **voluntary**. This does not mean that everything people do will be easy or fun, or that voluntary actions in this technical sense are precisely what the participants wished or are lauded by their friends and neighbors. But it does mean that they are not being coerced in the libertarian sense of the word—the actions are not the immediate result of property rights violations or threats of property rights violations.

The easiest way to envision a functioning libertarian society, then, may be to picture all human beings peacefully going about their business on a voluntary basis, with no one violating anyone else's property rights without fear of legal reprisal. The result would be a true free market; all interactions are un-coerced rather than government-mandated transactions.

At this point in the description of the philosophy, the newcomer to libertarianism typically has a positive reaction. Then, quickly, a look of worry comes over her face, as she thinks of all sorts of seemingly disastrous or insoluble situations that would arise in the absence (or near-absence) of government control.

Rather than live in fear, let's examine some of those situations and see how libertarians suggest they might be resolved.

PRACTICAL EXAMPLES

LIBERTARIANISM IS PRIMARILY A philosophy about what the *law* ought to be, not a philosophy of art or metaphysics or science. This doesn't mean that libertarians think such matters are unimportant, merely that libertarianism is a philosophy that focuses on a specific narrow subject. Adherents might and do have a wide range of opinions on other matters beyond the scope of the philosophy. In law, then, libertarianism can be thought of as forbidding three things (at least in a simplified model). As a practical matter, a libertarian law code forbids *assault*, *theft*, and *fraud*.

Fraud might be thought of as a species of theft—i.e., taking someone's property under false pretenses. Beyond that, in a strict libertarian sense, even assault can be thought of as a form of theft, since it entails using a very specific form of property—your body—without permission. Once

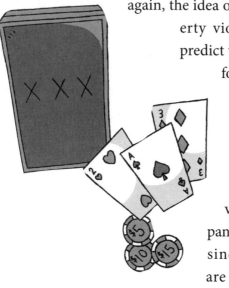

again, the idea of preventing property violations helps us predict what activities are forbidden in a libertarian society.

Note that libertarians would not consider a boxing match between voluntary participants a form of assault, since both parties are using their bodies as agreed in advance (assuming they're following the rules), no matter how violent it may look to third parties. Similarly, if our bodies are ours to do with as we choose, libertarians would have no *legal* objection to anyone becoming a stunt driver, mountain climber, drug user, reality TV show contestant, prostitute, or deep-sea diver. (Certain libertarians might give you a range of moral or psychological advice, some of it perhaps quite stern, about the wisdom of taking up any of these hobbies. It can be dangerous or stupid without being a crime.)

Because something is legal does not mean we must approve of it morally, just as something being immoral—such as saying something gratuitously rude to an elderly person passing on the street—does not necessarily mean that it should be illegal (unless it rises to the level of assault, theft, or fraud).

Libertarians contend that for anything to be rightly considered a crime, there ought to be an identifiable victim and some sort of measurable damages (or at least an attempt to cause damage). By contrast, so-called **"VIC-TIMLESS CRIMES,"** cannot properly be grounds for arrest in a libertarian society. If you use drugs (and do not physically injure anyone else in the process), watch pornography, sell products some people like and others don't, or have sex for money, and the only person complaining about these exchanges is the police officer, the politician, or some other third party who disapproves of your actions *but whose body or other property was not damaged by those actions*, there are no legitimate grounds for legal retaliation against you.

To put it in even clearer terms, there are no legitimate grounds for claiming you owe *restitution* to anyone. If you have physically harmed no one and taken no property from anyone, no harm or punishment ought to be initiated against you. This leaves most people with some big questions. Consider a few examples.

HOW DO WE PREVENT DRUG ADDICTION WITHOUT ARRESTING PEOPLE?

Just as most people use alcohol without becoming alcoholics, statistics suggest that most people who use other potentially addictive substances do so without becoming addicts. About half of Americans are estimated to have smoked marijuana at some point, for instance, but nowhere near that many are habitual or dysfunctional users. (Indeed marijuana is one substance that Americans are moving closer to legalizing.) In countries such as Portugal, where a broad range of drugs have been legalized, changing the law has made surprisingly little difference in the level of use.

This does not mean that drugs are harmless, or that we should be indifferent to the cases of addiction that do arise. However, just as we have found ways to discourage reckless alcohol consumption without jailing every drinker, so there are a number of voluntary methods at our disposal to deal with drug abuse—addiction counseling, psychotherapy, social pressure from friends and family, professional pressure from employers and co-workers, and moral and religious pressure throughout society. All of those methods would still exist under libertarian principles, plus more. In a society in which people are free to enter into whatever contracts they choose so long as they do not harm third parties, those who fear temptation of any kind could be encouraged to enter into strict, legally binding agreements that impose harsh penalties for straying.

Under current law, addicts sometimes receive welfare payments, must be kept on the job (under the rules of the Americans with Disabilities Act), or conceal their drug-taking activities for fear of being arrested. In a libertarian society, by contrast, employers would actually be freer to fire drug users or to enter into contracts with addictive personalities under which the employees can be fired if they engage in any drug use. Employers would still be free, as they often are now, to insist that employees pass drug tests. Suspicious spouses-to-be might even insist on prenuptial agreements that forbid the use of potentially addictive substances (and other kinds of behavior!).

In short, a whole array of social penalties and pressures could be brought to bear on individuals who pose a problem *without* subjecting the rest of society to the laws that put all of us, including casual users and non-users, at risk of being raided by police, shot in a melee between street gangs, beheaded by Mexican cartels, embroiled in Middle East opium wars or Central American coca-plant extermination, or sent to prison for years despite not having a truly debilitating drug habit. After all, it is the War on Drugs, not drug use itself, which has accounted for most of the violence and expense inflicted on society by America's "drug problem." If drugs were legal instead of being sold on the black market, the trade would be controlled by reputable companies that settle their disputes in court rather than by shadowy criminal organizations that settle their disputes with knives and pistols.

Never forget America's failed experiment in the 1920s with alcohol Prohibition, which, like our failed and expensive War on Drugs, produced violent criminal gangs eager to sell the products that legal businesses no longer could. A world in which drugs were legalized, like the world of legal alcohol in which we now live, would hardly be devoid of problems, but on balance it would likely be safer and more civil.

HOW DO WE PAY FOR PUBLIC SERVICES WITHOUT TAXES?

There is a bad habit among critics of libertarianism of imagining (or perhaps just pretending to believe) that if libertarians call for eliminating the participation of the government in activities X, Y, and Z (say, tree-planting, library construction, and opera), libertarians must want a world completely devoid of X, Y, and Z—perhaps even that libertarians *hate* X, Y, and Z and want to see them destroyed. On the contrary, since libertarians think government tends to do things badly and inefficiently, any perverse desire to destroy X, Y, and Z would encourage heavy government involvement in those activities!

PAY FOR MY CHILD'S EDUCATION!

BUT I DON'T EVEN KNOW YOU.

THE POWER TO TAX INVOLVES THE POWER TO DESTROY.

CHIEF JUSTICE JOHN MARSHALL IN
MCCULLOCH V. MARYLAND **(1819)**

Luckily, of course, there is another way to pay for things. It is the same method we use to pay for most everything in life—voluntarily. There is no inherent reason that user fees cannot be charged directly for virtually all the things the government now provides, from library subscriptions to road tolls to a competitive, fully stamp-funded postal service. The first instinct of a non-libertarian might be to lament that these services are currently "free" and that it would be a terrible loss, and an additional expense, to have to pay for them. Keep in mind, however, that all of these services are already being paid for by users, just in an involuntary, haphazard way in which there is little correlation between how much any given taxpayer pays for a particular service and how much use she gets out of it.

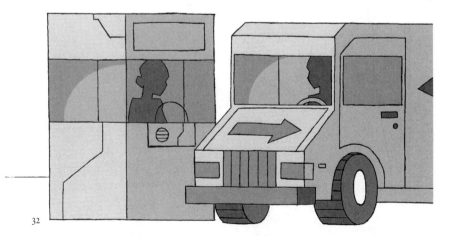

This means that government as currently constituted has little incentive or means to ensure that its resources are flowing to the services users want most. Politicians and other agents of government perpetually lament that their projects are dangerously underfunded—when have you ever heard a politician say that any vital program has too much money in its coffers and is going to give some back? So while public debate tends to hinge on the total amount being spent on government or on specific government projects, all government spending is a tragedy for those taxpayers who would have been made happier by other uses of the money.

A pedestrian in a rural Vermont town pays for highways in California that he may never use. A childless citizen pays for public schools to educate other people's children, often badly. When poor hip-hop fans pay sales tax for music, they are being forced by government to subsidize rich classical music fans who might be quite capable of paying for their own concert tickets. In short, it is virtually impossible, in a system that forces everyone to pay for everything, to be sure that *any-one* is actually coming out ahead in the flurry of trans-fers. Yet suggest putting an end to that flurry and letting *individuals* pay for the things they truly desire, and you will likely be condemned as a heartless, antisocial agent of greed with no sense of community.

Libertarians see that sort of accusation as pro-govern-ment propaganda—a defense of inefficiency masquerad-ing as moral concern.

Nor does defending the one-size-fits-all, monopolis-tic approach to government spending respect the diverse moral sensibilities of a vast citizenry. Under government authority, the pacifist will be forced to pay for foreign wars that may be morally dubious or futile. The traditional-ist will be forced to pay for a new modernist civic center. The animal welfare activist must fund the Department of Agriculture. The pro-life activist must subsidize abortion, and the pro-choice activist must provide public matching funds to the campaigns of pro-life politicians.

No wonder everyone ends up angry, convinced they are the ones being uniquely abused by government spending priorities. From a libertarian perspective, *everyone* is being abused by government.

A photograph distributed on the Internet mocked anti-government protesters by labeling all the objects around them that had been provided (generously, it was implied) by government, such as roads and stop signs. The impli-cation, of course, was that people who argue for less

government are often oblivious to all the features of contemporary life that are provided or protected by the state. On the contrary, libertarians are painfully aware that government creates or sustains at least half the services in modern American society. That is precisely the reason they think so many things, from bridge-building to driver's license renewals, are handled so badly.

Thus, libertarians argue, let all of it be replaced by free-market services, funded by willing users and provided by the producers best at keeping their individual customers satisfied.

SOUP
KITCHEN

SINCE 1913

**WHAT ABOUT
THE POOR?!**
....

CLOSED

Just as libertarians are routinely accused of not noticing
or appreciating how many things government funds, they
are routinely accused of not noticing or caring that there
are many poor people in the world. A society based on
user fees and market-based services, critics assume, is one
intended to provide endless luxuries to the rich while even
the most basic services remain out of reach for the poor.
The countless innocent people who would otherwise be
rescued by government, it is argued, fall through the cracks
of a heartless, Dickensian capitalist system.

But as free-market advocates have observed since Adam Smith did in the eighteenth century, government routinely harms the poor and helps the rich, even when attempting to do the opposite.

Government, always with the noblest-sounding intentions, routinely redistributes money "upward," away from the poor: when it taxes everyone to pay for retirement benefits for the elderly (who tend to have far more money than those just starting out in life); when through minimum wage laws it closes out crucial starter jobs that provide basic training at low wages for people who usually go on to bigger and better gigs later; when it forces business newcomers to pay expensive licensing fees or take long (sometimes irrelevant) classes to qualify for licenses to operate in certain businesses; when it imposes regulations that jibe smoothly with long-established and well-connected firms' methods of production but make it illegal for upstarts to do things in a new way; or when it imposes rent controls in some cities that keep rich elderly people hunkered down in cheap apartments while young new arrivals pound the pavement looking for units to rent at much higher rates to compensate landlords.

Starting roughly a century ago, government also took over the task of charity, displacing and destroying networks of mutual aid and private unemployment insurance run by poor people themselves, who had kept tabs on members and encouraged them with personal advice instead of checks from a faceless government welfare bureaucracy. In place of dignity, self-help, local knowledge, and autonomy, government offered the chance to become wards of the state.

PEOPLE NEED TO BE FED, MEDICATED, EDUCATED, CLOTHED, AND SHELTERED, AND IF WE'RE COMPASSIONATE WE'LL HELP THEM, BUT YOU GET NO MORAL CREDIT FOR FORCING OTHER PEOPLE TO DO WHAT YOU THINK IS RIGHT. THERE IS GREAT JOY IN HELPING PEOPLE, BUT NO JOY IN DOING IT AT GUNPOINT.

MAGICIAN AND AUTHOR PENN JILLETTE

But government has not merely competed with and displaced private charities. In many cases, it has actively attacked them by imposing restrictions on their activities that make it harder for them to do good. In the 1990s, for example, New York City told Mother Teresa, who eschewed modern technology, that her Missionaries of Charity could not open a homeless shelter in Manhattan unless it had elevators. Later, the City briefly cracked down on programs that gave food to the poor, saying they must provide only food that is free of trans-fats.

Libertarians generally do not argue that such steps are orchestrated, as some on the left might imagine, by secret cabals of right-wing regulators who hate the poor. These are just the usual bungles committed by government bureaucracies that churn out rules and have little interest in consequences. Private organizations used to dealing with customers and volunteers tend to have more heart and be a bit more thoughtful.

Meanwhile, overseas, the case for capitalism as a poverty-fighter is even stronger. Many nations keep their populations mired in near-starvation-level poverty by having the government run agriculture and most major business operations; by entangling private enterprises in endless regulatory red tape; and by failing to write clear, enforce-

able property rights into law. All of this makes it difficult for the average citizen to own property or equipment, to invest, to present collateral, or to make long-term contracts with any measure of confidence. Even in relatively booming countries such as China, the survival of one's factory may depend on the whims of Communist Party bosses instead of strong, defensible contracts. The less sure one is of one's property rights, the harder it is to plan long-term and think ambitiously.

By contrast, the period of relatively increased "globalization" and trade in the decade or two around the collapse of European Communism in the late 1980s and early 1990s saw the number of people on Earth who live in absolute poverty cut roughly in half, from about two billion to one billion. That still left a billion too many people in dire poverty, but it gave clear evidence that trade, not government control, is the best route out. Tariffs and trade quotas don't just get in the way of goods; they get in the way of the dreams of struggling customers and entrepreneurs who want to trade those goods, often driving them into the riskier world of the black market.

How do we control businesses that are violent or dangerous, such as prostitution?

Like many more conventional businesses, prostitution takes on its violent tendencies not from the nature of the business itself but largely *from the fact that the business is declared illegal by government.* Black markets of all kinds are filled with people who don't mind breaking the law and with others who are frightened to go to the authorities if they get robbed or beaten, lest they get arrested themselves.

As is often the case when government intervenes in the name of protecting people, it makes things worse for those people by outlawing one or more of their options and leaving them with even worse ones to choose from. Prostitution is certainly not a glamorous job, and it is not the first

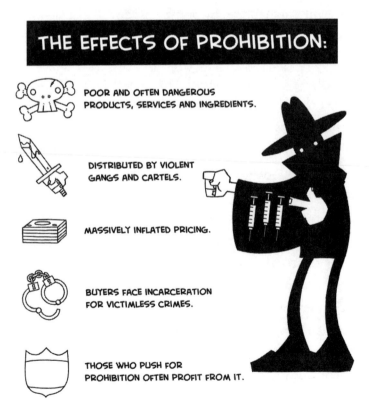

THE EFFECTS OF PROHIBITION:

POOR AND OFTEN DANGEROUS PRODUCTS, SERVICES AND INGREDIENTS.

DISTRIBUTED BY VIOLENT GANGS AND CARTELS.

MASSIVELY INFLATED PRICING.

BUYERS FACE INCARCERATION FOR VICTIMLESS CRIMES.

THOSE WHO PUSH FOR PROHIBITION OFTEN PROFIT FROM IT.

career choice of most who participate in it. But the same can be said of many other careers. If a man decides that his best career choice, given his skills and the pay being offered, is to become an assembly-line worker, we do not magically conjure better options for him by *outlawing* jobs as assembly-line workers!

Likewise, government does not help the prostitute (who for all we know greatly enjoys sex and has decided to go into her line of work for precisely that reason) by taking the job option away from her and dictating that she pursue some other line of work. It's certainly not clear that government helps her by putting her in jail instead of in a cheap motel. Most tragically of all, the government inhibits her willingness to call the police or a lawyer to defend her rights if beaten or robbed by a pimp or customer if she knows she will be arrested herself.

Businesses operating on the black market are also less able to advertise and compete on the basis of safety and health standards than are ones operating in the sunlight of legality. Legal brothels in Nevada, for example, tend to partner with doctors to ensure regular checkups for venereal diseases, not something for which there is any guarantee in areas where prostitution is illegal.

Like so many other thorny libertarian legal controversies, none of the above should be taken to mean that libertarians are obliged to approve *morally* of prostitution, only to permit it *legally*. Libertarians who are so inclined might still advise friends or the general public to consider other careers and to regard sex as a sacred bond best kept within the bounds of long-term monogamous relationships. But that's a psychological and cultural debate to be had between free individuals, not something to be decided by a government dispatching men with guns to put those on the losing side of the argument in jail cells.

Ultimately, if the prostitute and her customers are not injuring anyone else—which they are *less* likely to do if the whole operation is legally aboveboard—they may recognize the costs and benefits of their actions better than we do as third-party observers. At the very least, we are uncertain enough about their other options that we ought not to legally forbid their behavior.

WHAT IF SOMEONE BUYS THINGS ONLY TO DESTROY THEM?

To some, this may sound like a very odd question. But philosophies that people hear about for the first time may

inspire them to ask somewhat paranoid questions that they would not ask about more familiar belief systems.

Since owning property entails the right to do with it as you will, some non-libertarians fear, for instance, that a rich lunatic might buy all the trees in the world and set them on fire just for spite. As we will examine in greater detail in the next chapter, when contemplating such a

nightmare scenario, we would do well to ask how such a lunatic would become so wealthy in the first place that he is able to give all the previous tree owners in the world sufficient value in trade to hand over their trees.

Similarly, while we can imagine a scenario in which people conspire to buy all the land around one individual and then refuse to let him leave or to buy food, it is reasonable to wonder why selfish people would find it preferable to do that rather than, say, sell the person food or charge him a fee for use of an access corridor. In any event, it seems unlikely that such a scenario would arise with any frequency.

Generally speaking, one already has great leeway under current law to behave in a self-destructive, vandalizing, or highly annoying fashion. But there are powerful incentives not to do so with any regularity, at least if one wants to keep interacting with other people. It is not because of government that most people clean their apartments rather than try to set them on fire on a regular basis.

If someone wants to buy your old mansion just to tear it down and leave it an unused pile of rubble, he'll have to pay to do so, leaving you with a nice pile of cash, whether under the present legal system *or* a libertarian one. And if the person enjoys smashing it so much that he's willing to buy it, maybe that's the best use for the place. Some people buy balloons just to fill them with water, lob them, and burst them. If that makes them happy, why should the law intervene (assuming, as always, that they aren't harming anyone)?

The law, when it's being useful (and libertarian) keeps people from harming each other, but it does very little to keep people sane or to keep them from smashing things they own. That just isn't a very common desire.

In general, law—as opposed to spontaneous, personal advice tailored to nuanced local situations—should deal primarily with common social problems, such as reckless driving, pickpocketing, or breaking and entering.

Regardless of one's political philosophy, it is probably unwise to build a system of law around rare, strange scenarios such as the wasteful purchaser-and-burner of trees. Such a character is not likely to be a frequent problem. Like many other odd behaviors, this one can probably be safely tolerated by a free society, even if it makes little sense to most of us. That's the usual libertarian solution.

Ayn Rand—one of many libertarian thinkers we'll encounter later in this book but by no means the only one who has a say on this philosophy—argued that law and morality should not be built around "lifeboat scenarios," that is, strange emergency situations that are only remotely relevant to everyday life. Despite the prevalence of such emergency cases in philosophy class discussions, Rand may be right. After all, one could also argue against a more familiar political philosophy, such as democracy, by invoking some highly unlikely nightmare scenario. For example, what if 51% of the population in a pure democracy voted to kill the other 49%? With libertarianism as with democratic theory, it is only fair to address the basic, most likely scenarios first and to consider tricky hypothetical ones afterwards.

To understand the basics of the world as it operates according to libertarian thinking, it may be best to begin by examining the principles of free-market economics.

3 ECONOMICS

FROM A LIBERTARIAN PERSPECTIVE

ONE UNDENIABLE FACT ABOUT the world, even before you formulate any political theories about it, is that there are many people in it. No two of them are exactly alike, not even twins. Even within the same family, individuals may have widely divergent preferences.

You cannot know for sure what will make your neighbor happy, and he cannot know for sure what will make you happy. This means it is a good idea to adopt some system of social interaction that allows individuals to act on their own preferences. Presumably, when any person's preferences are thwarted—not just fleeting ones, but many of his preferences, systematically, over time—he will tend to be unhappy about it.

In economic terms, this means that "values are subjective"—not in the sense that phrase is sometimes used, as in moral rules being arbitrary. Rather, the strength of any individual's attachment to a certain course of action, or to a physical possession, will vary with that person's psychology and preferences. I might think a ticket to Tahiti is worth giving up $250 to possess; you might hate travel and think it's not worth a dime (unless perhaps you were planning to resell it). Even your own valuation of the ticket might change from week to week if, say, your schedule changes and you have more time for a vacation. There is no "correct" answer.

There is also no way to peer inside other people's minds and to know for sure how much value any individual places on something. In opinion surveys, which often serve as a basis for action by government, people notoriously give answers to questions about the value they place on things that are greatly at variance with their own subsequent spending. They may claim that the value of a local park is nearly infinite to them but reveal at a later date that they would not willingly pay even a $10 annual membership fee to use the park. People say a lot of things and, as the wonderful expression has it, it's better if someone "puts his money where his mouth is."

For a commercial transaction to occur (again, in the absence of force or fraud), the price has to be agreeable to both the buyer and the seller. Thus it is through the setting of prices in the marketplace (millions of them every day, in a completely decentralized way) that *revealed preferences* are discovered. We no longer have to take someone's word for it how much he values a sofa or a cupcake. Now we know. Prices at most stores in the industrialized world are set at what the owner thinks is the likely amount customers will be willing to pay—enough of them to make it profitable to bring that amount of product to market.

At the same time, however, there is something especially useful and informative about the practice—more common in informal markets and the developing world—of haggling. Haggling over the price of anything makes it clear that both parties have preferences that may be adjustable with negotiation. The price of an item is not some fixed, objective amount, like physical size or mass.

To some, the subjective nature of economic valuation may sound disquieting, as though it renders the world more chaotic and complicated. People in medieval times thought there must be some correct "just" price that should be charged, and this superstitious notion echoes in our own day whenever the government claims that price controls should be imposed or that the price of something has risen (or fallen) "without reason." The real reason is always the interplay of the sellers' preference to sell for the highest possible price and the buyers' preference to buy at the lowest possible price. Neither side quite gets their wish, and no third party can say which side should.

And yet buying and selling in a world of diverse preferences and subjective valuations also has a wonderful, happy side effect!

If the value of any given item offered for sale (a book, for example) is really its subjective value *to someone*, then when it gets freely traded for something else (a hat, say), it means that the person who started out with the book must have valued the hat more *and vice versa*. In other words, it is possible—even likely—that both parties will be happier after the trade than they were before. Indeed we should assume that, absent force or fraud, this is precisely the case.

Understood in these terms, the transaction does not produce a "winner" and a "loser" (or an "exploiter" and an "exploited," to put it in pessimistic Marxist-influenced terms). Instead, each trade is a case of ***mutually***

beneficial exchange. In all of libertarian theory, mutually beneficial exchange is perhaps the single most important idea for understanding social reality. Rather than a world in which there is a fixed quantity of already-distributed goods—and a fixed, unchanging amount of happiness—the possibility of mutually beneficial exchange posits a world in which constant trading between billions of ever-changing pairs of individuals or parties can make everyone better off than they were the moment before the trade.

Better yet, because the subjective improvement in well-being is judged by each party to any trade, there is no need for an outside party—whether a bystander or a central

authority—to judge from afar whether the "correct" trades are occurring. In other words, barring unusual circumstances that may make it impossible for certain individuals to act upon their real preferences (because they are mentally ill or too young to make competent decisions, for example), all trades can be assumed to be good in the minds of those voluntarily engaging in them.

This doesn't mean that we never change our minds after a trade or regret that we couldn't find an even better deal. It also doesn't mean that we will continue to value the item purchased forever, as our preferences change over time or in different social contexts. Generally speaking, however, each of us is best able to judge whether we are getting a satisfactory deal *by making the exchange rather than not making the exchange.* The advice of experts and friends is always welcome—that's what consumer magazines, product chat rooms, and warnings from elderly relatives are for.

But if both parties to a trade remain convinced the transaction is beneficial, no one in the world has the power to read their minds and say with certainty that they are wrong. Thus, it is generally a bad idea for a third party to use violence, coercion, or mandate to forbid the exchange or to force the two parties to engage in some other exchange that they don't want and don't value.

In reality, libertarians argue, government interferes with trade—resulting in a reduction in overall happiness—virtually every time it acts (with the possible exception of its purely defensive, rights-protecting functions). In essence, government, despite its appearance of having thousands of functions, really does only two things: forbid people from making the trades they want, and force them to make trades they don't want.

The idea that government "helps" us somehow is, in strict libertarian terms, a mere superstition.

THE POSITIVE TESTIMONY OF HISTORY
IS THAT THE STATE INVARIABLY HAD ITS
ORIGIN IN CONQUEST AND CONFISCATION.
NO PRIMITIVE STATE KNOWN TO HISTORY
ORIGINATED IN ANY OTHER MANNER.

ALBERT JAY NOCK, *OUR ENEMY, THE STATE*

The biggest implication of the concept of mutually beneficial exchange between two parties is that virtually *all* trade may be seen as a net benefit to the participants. (Again, this assumes that they are trading without fraud and without violating the property rights of third parties, as they would be, for example, if they were contracting to assassinate a third party or damaging a third party's property by polluting it.)

Put in more sweeping, societal terms, libertarians hold that all regulatory interference with trade—regulation, tariffs, price controls, government subsidies to favored industries, taxes on sales or income, licensing fees, etc.—tends to *reduce* the happiness of the otherwise beneficially trading parties. That makes *laissez-faire* capitalist policies, a bare minimum of interference with markets and property rights, the natural complement to libertarian philosophical premises. Crucially, since no one is seen as having a right to violate another person's property rights under a libertarian system, laissez-faire does *not* imply, as leftist critics often allege, "rule" by corporations or the rich. Everyone's rights are the same—namely property rights—and everyone is free to engage in trade.

Indeed, in a laissez-faire system, unlike a big-government system, resources will tend to flow to—and make rich—only those who provide valuable services to others. In an environment in which all exchanges are voluntary, political pull and connections to government will be of little avail. *Resource allocation* will tend to be efficient,

where efficiency is defined by the happiness of willing participants as revealed by their trades. (Naturally, there will be ambiguous or troubling cases under any system, and laissez-faire capitalism is no exception; we will examine some of those later.)

Just as libertarians reject the Marxist notion that every exchange has an "exploiting" and an "exploited" participant in favor of the idea of mutually beneficial exchange, so libertarians reject the idea that profit is a bad thing. On the contrary, if the human race benefits from transferring resources from lower-valued to higher-valued uses, *profits are a vital signaling device* that someone is producing things that people want, that somewhere things are being done a better way.

I'M SORRY, SIR, BUT YOUR FACTORY IS IN DIRECT COMPETITION WITH ONE OWNED BY THE COUSIN OF A CITY OFFICIAL. WE'LL HAVE TO SHUT IT DOWN!

Since most people respond to positive incentives—whether in the form of money, acclaim, or any other metric *they individually consider important*—profits are an important means of incentivizing people to imitate what works (i.e., producing what makes others happy) and to avoid what doesn't. Profits are an indication that some person or organization is especially good at moving resources to higher-valued uses.

A properly functioning market, in other words, is an infinitely multidirectional feedback loop of ever-increasing happiness. This hardly means that things are perfect in a free market. Nature inflicts horrors. People periodically violate the rules by stealing or committing assault. The desperate needs of certain individuals and any range of side effects go unforeseen. But the tendency is for every pair—or multidirectional set—of interacting people to keep seeking improvement, to keep moving in the direction of individuals satisfying their preferences as best they can in the context of other people's willingness to interact.

Government, seen in this light, does not merely make occasional mistakes. It does not merely waste money some of the time. From this point of view, government is the constant, all-pervading, systematic violator of property rights and the "misallocator" of resources. It takes resources away from the highest-valued uses to which free individuals

otherwise would put them and steers them toward lower-valued uses. Government constantly destroys happiness.

The defender of government, or "statist," might interject that a number of important tasks may never be performed if left to the unfettered marketplace. To most people, in fact, this seems like an obvious danger of laissez-faire capitalism. But we must stop to ask this question: How should we determine that tasks are "important" in the first place if not by letting people choose them freely in the marketplace, especially in light of people's willingness to engage in mutually beneficial exchanges?

The true test is revealed preference, or financial commitment. If asked in a survey whether they think having a 20-foot solid-gold statue of Benjamin Franklin in the middle of town would be valuable, many people might well say yes. However, if they were invited to pay for the statue through charitable contributions, to buy a ticket to view it, or even to invest in it and charge admission, many would be less favorably inclined. In other words, there would be far less interest in the statue when people imagine paying for it themselves than when they imagine forcing *other* people to pay for it. Having unlimited access to other people's resources (hypothetically) and not feeling guilty about it has a tendency to make people favor all sorts of "important" projects instead of *economizing* and putting resources into the things they truly value. Everything seems worth doing when you don't have to imagine giving up anything for it.

THE TRAGEDY OF THE COMMONS

Another way of looking at the problem is to think of it as what the twentieth-century ecologist Garrett Hardin called "the tragedy of the commons." Hardin was no libertarian, but he identified an economic dilemma central to libertarian thinking: the fact that things held in common, owned by everyone and no one, will tend to get used inefficiently, often overused or under-maintained, with each user (intentionally or not) being slightly more likely to shirk the duties of maintenance and hope the next person will take care of it.

Economists have pointed to the overgrazing of a shared meadow by shepherds as a classic example. Admittedly, not all of these economists have reached the libertarian conclusion that it is best to avoid having a commons or other public property in the first place. Hardin himself saw the tragedy of the commons primarily as a reason

STOP EATING THAT
UNHEALTHY FOOD AT ONCE!
I DON'T WANT TO PAY FOR
YOUR HEALTH CARE DOWN
THE ROAD!

to institute strict regulations on the use of the commons. Even a libertarian can readily agree that, in an *inescapable* commons, some sort of regulation may be best. The deeper question, however, is whether the problem can be avoided altogether by avoiding the establishment of a commons to begin with, that is, by establishing private property rights whenever possible. (Even fishing rights, river usage rights, and "air corridors" have been parceled out at times in ways that closely mimic property rights in fluid bodies.)

One of the founding European settlements of what would become the United States, Plymouth Colony in Massachusetts, first attempted communal farming on the assumption

THEN DON'T.

that it was the most fitting economic arrangement for a unified religious community. Growing hungry and despairing of the experiment, however, the settlers soon switched to individual family plots, which proved far more fruitful. As the governor of the colony observed, the farmers were far more industrious in tending family plots than they were working the communal grounds. The lesson would be relearned, with a much higher body count, by communist regimes in the twentieth century after their attempts at collective farming.

The problem is not unique to agriculture or land, though there is a subset of the libertarian movement called "free-market environmentalism" that focuses on the ways in which government stewardship of the natural environment routinely fails, whereas private property helps sustain resources and minimize pollution (contrary to the anti-capitalist caricatures common to mainstream or leftist environmental thinking). Any shared, pooled resource becomes subject to the same sorts of inefficiencies, since

its value to any individual users is obscured.

The same is true, libertarians maintain, if any significant portion of national income is taken from individual owners and put into a single collective fund located in Washington, D.C., to be parceled out by government employees instead of changing hands via the millions of transactions that would otherwise have occurred between hundreds of millions of individual Americans.

The problem is exacerbated, argue libertarians, by the fact that government can tout its visible accomplishments—such as a new military base or that statue of Benjamin Franklin—and possibly produce (or respond to) a small but vocal constituency for those specific projects, while the costs of the projects are widely and almost undetectably distributed among the entire population.

This does not mean, it must be emphasized, that there has been a gain without any loss. More likely it means that the benefits are weighed and the costs overlooked, and that projects are undertaken at a net loss fiscally and in terms of human happiness. This problem is summarized by economists as the dilemma of "concentrated benefits and dispersed costs." It is a perfect formula for turning a pool of collective resources—such as all the money in Washington—into a trough for lobbyists, the agents of the people who *receive* the concentrated benefits, rather than a pooled source of happiness and well-being for the wider ocean of inattentive taxpayers.

Humanity did not start out wrestling with subtle issues such as these, of course. It spent millennia worrying about kings, empires, soldiers, slaves, magical powers, and hunting or farming enough food to survive. But the core issues of concern to libertarians, such as economic productiv-

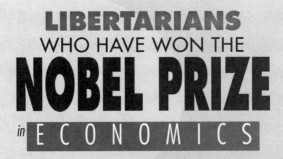

LIBERTARIANS
WHO HAVE WON THE
NOBEL PRIZE
in ECONOMICS

Friedrich August von Hayek, 1974 (jointly with Gunnar Myrdal)

"for their pioneering work in the theory of money and economic fluctuations and for their penetrating analysis of the interdependence of economic, social and institutional phenomena"

According to the website of the libertarian Cato Institute, "A frequent lament amongst libertarians is the number of talented individuals who never received the prize. Fritz Machlup, for example, was a leading theorist in the pure theory of international trade. Ludwig von Mises was one of the most pioneering economists of the twentieth century. Lord P. T. Bauer contributed vast scholarship to the literature of development economics. Gordon Tullock, Buchanan's partner in the creation of Public Choice, has done pioneering work in the field of rent seeking."

Milton Friedman, 1976

"for his achievements in the fields of consumption analysis, monetary history and theory and for his demonstration of the complexity of stabilization policy"

James M. Buchanan, Jr., 1986

"for his development of the contractual and constitutional bases for the theory of economic and political decision-making"

Gary S. Becker, 1992

"for having extended the domain of microeconomic analysis to a wide range of human behaviour and interaction, including nonmarket behaviour"

Vernon L. Smith, 2002

"for having established laboratory experiments as a tool in empirical economic analysis, especially in the study of alternative market mechanisms"

ity and the tension between freedom and tyranny, were almost always present.

A look at developments in recent centuries helps to explain how libertarianism as a distinctive, conscious philosophy finally arose. Along the way, we will meet some of the most famous economists, philosophers, political writers, and even politicians to espouse libertarian views.

4

CLASSICAL LIBERALISM

EVEN CHIMPANZEES ARE CAPABLE of being outraged if other chimpanzees take their food, so the basic impulses to defend property and to resist assault (if not our conceptual frameworks for them) no doubt predate human history. The earliest human writings contain condemnations of thieves, tales of murderers, and warnings about tyrannical kings. The specific philosophical formulation of these ideas, which led historically to what we recognize as libertarianism, arose to a large degree in England.

ANGLO ROOTS

Libertarians today hardly give a blanket endorsement to every un-libertarian aspect of English history, from aristocracy to imperialism. But even when bad things were happening there—and sometimes *because* bad things were happening there—good ideas were also arising.

Monarchical overreach led to political responses, such as the imposition by nobles of **THE MAGNA CARTA** on King John in 1215, arguably the first written document to explicitly limit a sovereign's power.

> TO ALL FREE MEN OF OUR KINGDOM WE HAVE ALSO GRANTED, FOR US AND OUR HEIRS FOR EVER, ALL THE LIBERTIES WRITTEN OUT BELOW, TO HAVE AND TO KEEP FOR THEM AND THEIR HEIRS, OF US AND OUR HEIRS.
>
> **MAGNA CARTA**

The mid-seventeenth-century English movement known as **THE LEVELLERS**—a term first used as an insult, implying that adherents wanted to tear everything down—took the opportunity during the instability of the English Civil War to publish pamphlets calling for broader suffrage, equality before the law, and religious toleration.

Just prior to England's so-called Glorious Revolution of 1688, philosopher John Locke wrote his *Two Treatises of*

Government, which were published just after the Revolution, in 1689, as a vindication of it. In them, Locke argued that rulers must have the consent of the governed and that the governed retain the right to overthrow a government that oppresses them, much as the Parliamentarians arguably had by replacing King James II with the Dutch king William III.

Key ideas from Locke—such as the right to revolt and the moral claim to ownership of previously unowned land *if you mix your labor with it*—went on to have a profound influence on mainstream politics and libertarian thinking alike. There was no distinctively libertarian tradition as of yet, and Locke is often regarded as a

Biography:
JOHN LOCKE (1632–1704)

A major figure of the early English Enlightenment, philosopher John Locke was no libertarian by today's standards—endorsing both monarchy and slavery—but still an important influence on a bundle of ideas that shaped the history of libertarian thought.

Considered a founder of the classical liberal tradition, he shared with many other writers in that tradition a tendency to link scientific curiosity about the workings of the individual mind, an economic perspective on national well-being, and a natural rights framework for thinking about morals and politics that mirrored both English legal tradition and contemporary Newtonian thinking about laws of the physical universe.

Locke was a progenitor of the empiricist notion (largely fallen out of favor thanks to modern knowledge of biology and instincts) that we are born with a mind that is a blank slate—or *tabula rasa*—to be molded solely by sense impressions and reason.

Despite writing a monarchical and slavery-respecting constitution for the Carolinas colony in the New World, he was also a pivotal early defender of social contract theory and the idea that the governed have a right to overthrow oppressive rulers—views vindicated by the 1688 Glorious Revolution in England and the 1776 Declaration of Independence in America. Locke fled to the Netherlands five years prior to the Glorious Revolution, suspected (probably falsely) of involvement in a conspiracy to assassinate the king and his brother.

Locke's articulation of something akin to the labor theory of value is less respected today than his use of the concept of supply and demand. His exploration of the vexing question of how previously unsettled land can come to be rightfully owned still influences economic philosophy debates. The question was urgent for a nation sending both capitalist settlers and imperialist military missions abroad. Locke concluded—befitting an era with growing respect for yeoman farmers and decreasing respect for conquerors—that one must "mix one's labor" with the land in some way to make it one's own.

Much as his *Two Treatises of Civil Government* (1689) argued for a contractarian view of government, his *Letter Concerning Toleration*, published the same year, was an important early argument for religious tolerance after centuries of periodic sectarian strife and routine government suppression of disfavored sects.

founder of **"CLASSICAL LIBERALISM."** That phase of liberal philosophy, existing roughly in the eighteenth and nineteenth centuries, emphasized individual liberty and free markets rather than group conflict and welfare states, as emphasized in twentieth-century **"MODERN LIBERALISM."**

Locke's views were by no means synonymous with later libertarianism. One of history's odder footnotes is that he actually wrote a constitution to be used in the Americas even before writing his *Two Treatises*. In 1669, while Locke was serving as secretary to England's Chancellor of the Exchequer, the Earl of Shaftesbury, the Province of Carolina (a vast area of land stretching from what is now Virginia to Florida) adopted "Fundamental Constitutions" written by Locke that were distinctly non-libertarian in character. While displaying the rationalizing tendencies of a philosopher, Locke tried to codify a system of aristocracy and strong protections for slave owners instead of a system of liberty.

Luckily for history, the colonists ignored his plans and within a few years had abandoned his official constitutions for local laws that were at least a bit closer to straightforward property rights and helped facilitate booming commerce. Slavery, of course, would endure another two centuries.

THE AMERICAN WAY

A full century after Locke's failed Carolina constitutions, the pamphleteers of the **AMERICAN REVOLUTION** (beginning in 1775) emerged as more recognizable forebears of contemporary libertarian thinking, even if they did not espouse a precise philosophy.

The Revolution, steeped in the individual rights principles of English common law and the natural rights ideas of eighteenth-century Enlightenment philosophers, was a coalition of often bitterly opposed factions, but it did promote the idea of limiting government and the Lockean idea that the people have the right to overthrow an oppressive regime.

[G]IVE ME LIBERTY OR GIVE ME DEATH!

PATRICK HENRY, AMERICAN REVOLUTIONARY

Jefferson, though himself a slave owner, made distinctly Lockean-sounding arguments in the **DECLARATION OF INDEPENDENCE**, presented to the public on July 4, 1776:

We hold these truths to be self-evident, that all men are created equal, that they are endowed by their Creator with certain unalienable Rights, that among these are Life, Liberty and the pursuit of Happiness.

That to secure these rights, Governments are instituted among Men, deriving their just powers from the consent of the governed,
   That whenever any Form of Government becomes destructive of these ends, it is the Right of the People to alter or to abolish it, and to institute new Government, laying its foundation on such principles and organizing its powers in such form, as to them shall seem most likely to effect their Safety and Happiness.

News of the American Revolution—in truth a world war, thanks to fighting across the British Empire involving the American-allied French—inspired rebellious thinkers around the globe.

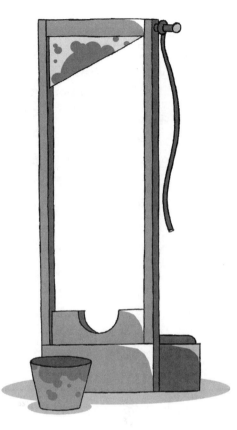

Though today we see a sharp contrast between the American Revolution, which was essentially a war of secession (from England), and the French Revolution, which aimed at a radical internal transformation of society (and was thus in some ways a model for later totalitarians, not libertarians), the two revolutions were often seen as allied at the time. Both **THOMAS PAINE** and **THOMAS JEFFERSON** wrote of the revolutions as parts of a common cause, explicitly founded on the Rights of Man.

In addition, libertarians tend to value *subsidiarity* in government, especially the rights of states over the more distant, centralized federal government. That is doubly true in the United States, where the federal government came into existence only as a compact between the individual states. Indeed, much as libertarians tend to revere the government-limiting framers of the **U.S. CONSTITUTION** and the writers of *The Federalist Papers* who advocated the Constitution's adoption (James Madison, Alexander

Hamilton, and John Jay), some point out that the so-called Anti-Federalists, who opposed the Constitution, were even *more* libertarian in some of their arguments.

To avoid all the problems that come with a strong central government—including the replacement of free-market banking and competing private currencies by a central bank, later the Federal Reserve, and a single government-printed currency—perhaps we should have stuck with the looser Articles of Confederation. One can contemplate that intriguing possibility while still admiring the brilliance of the U.S. Constitution.

THE PHYSIOCRATS AND ADAM SMITH

Throughout the eighteenth century, a school of French economists known as the Physiocrats also wrote about the (science-like) quest for the natural laws governing commerce and prosperity, hoping to see them reflected in man-made laws.

In the same year as the Declaration of Independence, which focused on politics, a publication of comparable importance in the history of economics appeared: Adam Smith's book *The Wealth of Nations*. Smith is quite moderate by today's libertarian standards, listing many rule-setting and standards-enforcing functions he thinks government should perform and endorsing something akin to Marx's labor theory of value (in contrast to the user-determined valuations described in the prior chapter).

Smith was moderate even compared to the Physiocrats in some ways. He wrote for an audience that accepted some rather nationalistic premises about the value of enhancing the royal treasury, premises that often led his contemporaries to think like corporatists (advocates of government-licensed trade rather than true free trade).

By the standards of the day, however, Smith was a powerful new voice in favor of lowering tariffs and permitting free trade. He helped make many inside and outside of government aware for the first time of the benefits to be gained from permitting buyers and sellers in the market

Biography:
ADAM SMITH (1723 –1790)

Part of the eighteenth-century Scottish

Enlightenment, Smith studied at University of Glasgow and Oxford and taught logic and later moral philosophy at the former. Among the many intellectuals he considered friends and welcomed to his home for conversations on philosophy and politics was David Hume. Smith was a member of the scientific advisory body known as the Royal Society of London and a founding member of the similar Royal Society of Edinburgh. He is best known for two books, *Theory of Moral Sentiments* (1759) and *Wealth of Nations* (1776); he also wrote a history of astronomy and many essays collected posthumously.

Though sometimes described as clashing works, his two best-known books depict humans as responding somewhat predictably to incentives. The former work describes the beneficial reputational and emotional effects of good behavior and being a good person. The latter work describes the myriad benefits from leaving people free to pursue commerce for their own enrichment. In this, his thinking resembled that of the free-market Physiocrat school of thinkers in France.

Many of Smith's premises about the benefits of global trade in the absence of tariffs and other regulatory barriers are now taken for granted by most market-oriented thinkers. In his own time, however, he had to fight widespread lobbying by "merchants and manufacturers." It was commonly thought not only that monarchs should award commissions and licenses to a handful of well-connected major businesses, but that amassing as much gold as possible in the national treasury tended to be beneficial. Smith argued in terms of the benefits to all of those doing the buying and selling, including the poor, instead of the effects on the royal treasury.

He viewed government as fit to engage in industrial activities or to grant monopoly licenses to companies engaged in industrial activities only of the most predictable and routine sort, which he took to include such tasks as canal-building and irrigation, as well as defense.

At a young age, Smith was prone to engage in imaginary conversations; as an adult, he become distracted while contemplating deep subjects, reportedly wandering long distances or ignoring his surroundings. A scientific systematizer yet somewhat absent-minded, he might have been regarded in a later era as the quintessential "nerd" or perhaps even mildly autistic.

Mocked for indifference to tradition by the Tories of his day, he would be an icon for both conservatives and libertarians in the twentieth century. Beginning in the late 1960s, some free-market advocates took to wearing neckties with Smith's likeness on them.

to pursue their self-interest. As he famously wrote, "It is not from the benevolence of the butcher, the brewer, or the baker that we expect our dinner, but from their regard to their own interest." Just as few workers would get out of bed each day if they stopped receiving paychecks, so very little production would occur if we eliminated the profit motive. Moreover, he argued, it is beneficial for those adept at brewing or baking to be rewarded through profits for their productive work. Letting them work at the tasks that are most remunerative for them creates efficiency through the specialization of labor. Not everyone should be baking pies. Not everyone is good at making wagon wheels.

Those who insist on making wagon wheels that are shoddy risk being sued and thus having their insurance premiums go up. So, even in the complete absence of regulation, there is an incentive not to harm customers. And killing them, of course, undermines repeat business. Despite constant leftist complaints that businesses don't "care" about their customers, they don't really need to, aside from the intense interest they must take to keep them as happy customers.

On an international scale, Smith was also one of the first defenders of what we would now call global trade. He argued against protectionist measures that keep inefficient local industries protected from global competition in the short run but, by robbing people of the best goods and most efficient production methods available, that make everyone poorer in the long run.

DAVID RICARDO AND FREDERIC BASTIAT

Inspired by *Wealth of Nations* and heavily influenced by the French Physiocrats, the English economist David Ricardo further refined the idea of benefits from global trade into the notion of "comparative advantage." That is, it is most efficient for humanity as a whole if goods tend to be produced by those most adept at creating them (as judged by purchasers balancing cost and quality). This may mean that some nations (or companies) simply leave cloth-making or shipbuilding to others and purchase the goods from them. Just as each of us would be unimaginably poor (and probably soon dead) if we each tried to make all our own

lightbulbs, medicine, or food from scratch, so too each nation is impoverished if—because of its own trade barriers or those erected by others nations—it has to do everything itself.

Even today, this important lesson—all gained from the specialization of labor that Smith observed and the comparative advantages that Ricardo observed—has not sunk into the minds of many politicians and activists. The message is lost on policy makers who regularly call for import quotas to protect local steel, sugar, or textile manufacturers; bans on "shoddy" foreign goods (that Americans want to buy) or goods not made by American labor unions; or protective tariffs for "infant industries" in developing nations. All of these measures make goods harder to produce and thus more expensive, which is no kindness to consumers who have to pay higher prices or go without.

In the first half of the nineteenth century, French essayist, political economist, and politician Frederic Bastiat was a particularly good public communicator of economic concepts and hewed more closely than earlier figures to what we would now recognize as a consistent libertarian philosophy. Bastiat helped to popularize criticism of what is now known as the "broken window fallacy" in economics: the dangerous belief that if work is created by destroying something (or making some task more difficult) it is a net benefit to humanity.

As Bastiat recognized, work may be created for window-makers by smashing windows (or for hand-loom operators by limiting which products can legally be made in modern textile factories, as India does), but the resources poured into window repair could otherwise have been spent on more productive activities, such as buying clothing, art,

Biography:
FREDERIC BASTIAT (1801-1850)

The son of a businessman in southern France, Bastiat observed the Napoleonic Wars as a child, worked for his uncle's export business as a teen, and as a young man inherited wealth from his grandfather that allowed him to pursue intellectual pursuits including philosophy, politics, and economics. In his thirties, he served as a justice of the peace and member of the county assembly. In his final years, he served as a member of France's national legislature, created in the wake of the continent-wide revolutions of 1848–1850.

Bastiat was known for the clarity, wit, and forceful arguments of his essays on economic policy and formulated many of the best arguments against regulation and aspects of the welfare state even before most Europeans were conscious of a modern regulatory/welfare state arising. Writing works such as *Economic Sophisms* (1845) in England, more receptive to laissez-faire than his native country, Bastiat demolished prevailing anti-market assumptions. Many of his arguments—and many reprints of his essays—have endured into the twenty-first century.

One of his most famous arguments was a dissection of the "broken window fallacy," the idea that an act of destruction (such as a war or building fire) benefits humans by increasing the need for economic activity. As he explained, distinguishing between "What Is Seen and What Is Not Seen," that activity merely ends up being performed in place of other, even more desirable and productive actions that might have been undertaken in the absence of the destructive incident.

In a fashion resembling Jonathan Swift, Bastiat expertly took his opponents' arguments to their logical conclusion, as in his parodic petition of the candlemakers against unfair competition from the sun — the ultimate protectionist folly.

In his short 1850 book *The Law*, published just before his death, Bastiat described a free society and the contrary temptation to plan all aspects of society. He foresaw many of the dehumanizing aspects of twentieth-century totalitarianism by extrapolating from the growing spider-web of regulations in the French Republic of his own day. He also saw that big government can arise from multiple philosophical traditions, criticizing the republican regulations of his time, the schemes of the rising socialist movements, and the political fantasies of conservative admirers of the Greco-Roman classics.

He is said to have murmured "the truth" as he died from tuberculosis at age 49. In the early twenty-first century, the libertarian Reason Foundation awarded an annual prize in Bastiat's name for the most effective free-market arguments in journalism.

or oats for horses. Make-work projects merely divert time and money from the things which people would really have valued most.

Two centuries later, even the Nobel Prize-winning economist Paul Krugman did not seem to understand this point, as he mused publicly on more than one occasion that something like a devastating alien invasion would be a boon to a sluggish economy. By contrast, Krugman won the Nobel for his work in the 1970s on the rather free-market and Ricardo-like observation that international trade

WOOO! LOOK AT ALL THESE JOBS I'M CREATING!

produces benefits even between nations with no obvious comparative advantages over each other, by offering consumers greater variety.

CONSERVATISM AND EDMUND BURKE

Since a relatively young philosophy such as libertarianism inherits many older influences, it can be difficult to tease out which historical influences were crucial. It is generally agreed, however, that libertarianism is an outgrowth of the relatively laissez-faire, individualistic, constitutionalist "classical" phase of liberalism. But is it also indebted to conservatism?

The easiest way to trace the influence of other philosophies on libertarianism is generally to trace the extent to which those other philosophies embraced free markets. While markets have remained a core value for libertarianism, other philosophies have treated markets as tools to be used or discarded depending on political circumstances.

So, for instance, market advocates often found themselves allied with leftist or anarchist radicals in the nineteenth century, when the legal privileges of monarchs and aristocrats were perceived as the common foe. In nineteenth-century England, for instance, the conservatives, or Tories, often opposed free-market reforms on the grounds that traditional and agrarian communities would be disrupted by trade. Liberals, including **ECONOMISTS OF THE MANCHESTER SCHOOL,** saw that transformation

as a good thing, though by the twentieth century those who called themselves liberals would adopt increasingly socialist and welfare-statist policy prescriptions.

Yet even back in the eighteenth century, the man often regarded as the founding conservative writer of modern times, Irish-born member of the British Parliament Edmund Burke, showed a distinct libertarian streak. (Burke is sometimes even credited with the first book-length defense of anarchism, his youthful and likely semi-satirical *Vindication of Natural Society.*) There is no question that his mature arguments were rooted in reverence for tradition rather than property rights per se, but that very deference to tradition made him skeptical, as any libertarian also must be, of the totalitarian, all-transforming streak in the French Revolution, as explained in his book *Reflections on the Revolution in France* (1790).

Burke certainly recognized the dangers of attempting to politically plan all of society (a warning that would be echoed in the twentieth century by libertarian economist Friedrich Hayek). At the same time, though, Burke was a supporter of the American Revolution, seeing it as a natural evolution of local mores away from the parental influ- ence of the mother country. Burke was also a Whig, though he was more hon- ored by Tories in the centuries to come.

JOHN STUART MILL

If Edmund Burke embodied tensions within conservatism, a later Member of Parliament, mid-nineteenth-century philosopher John Stuart Mill (mentioned at the start of this book) encapsulated the changing nature of liberalism. A son of the Scottish historian and philosopher James Mill, one of the founders of the philosophy of utilitari- anism, J.S. Mill believed that all moral codes throughout history had been *approx- imations* of the true moral ideal of seeking to maximize human happiness. Happiness is the one goal for which no further purpose need be sought, Mill argued. Unlike other rough metrics, such as "solidarity" or "adherence to custom" or "equality," happiness is its own justification and undermining it is manifestly destructive.

Unlike some earlier utilitarians who believed in trying to assess the happiest outcome on a case-by-case basis, the Victorian and staid Mill saw the need for predictable, consistent moral rules and laws to avoid constant self-serving disagreement over which course of action is the moral one. That stance made him what would now be called a "rule" utilitarian as opposed to an "act" (that is, one action at a time) utilitarian.

By Mill's line of reasoning, we might also overcome the apparent clash between rights-oriented and utilitarian thinking. Rights may be thought of as extremely valuable practices or rules that should not be violated lightly, rather than as metaphysical entities that trump all concern for consequences.

Steeped in the laissez-faire economic views of his day, Mill initially believed that strict adherence to property rights, free markets, and limited government constituted the rules best suited to produce a happy society, as explained in his 1859 book *On Liberty* and his series of 1861 essays that became the book *Utilitarianism*. Mill was not always confident, though, that individual choice without substantial moral and intellectual guidance would lead to happy outcomes. Indeed he made exceptions to the rule that markets should be unregulated. For example, he advocated government subsidies for education, which he deemed a kind of prerequisite for happy decision-making. Early in his life, when he served as a colonial administrator in India via the East India Company, he believed the British Empire ought to guide developing nations to cultural and political maturity through what he called "benevolent despotism."

Mill also favored a subtle combination of feminist open-mindedness and Victorian strict morals as a means of avoiding either backwardness or hedonistic shallowness that might impair careful long-term planning and thus long-term happiness. He recognized the superiority of sophisticated joys to fleeting indulgence. Toward the end of his career, his paternalistic streak (and some argue the influence of his wife) led Mill to share the mounting late-nineteenth-century liberal enthusiasm for the potential of the state to enhance human well-being, and his adherence to laissez-faire diminished.

SLAVERY AND THE AMERICAN CIVIL WAR

While Mill was publishing his most famous works about liberty and happiness, across the Atlantic in the United States, one of the most anti-libertarian insti-

> WHAT AM I SUPPOSED TO DO IF I CAN'T DENY YOU THE RIGHT OF SELF-OWNERSHIP? PAY PEOPLE A WAGE BASED ON MARKET DEMAND? I'D BE RUINED!

tutions in human history—slavery—was entering its death throes in the Civil War.

History rarely presents us with a situation that is an unalloyed good or evil, and the American Civil War is sufficiently complex that it still causes arguments within (and about) the libertarian movement in the twenty-first century. There is no question that **THE ABOLITIONISTS** tended to make highly recognizable libertarian arguments, sometimes relying on the axiomatic idea of *self-ownership* that would be taken as a philosophical starting point by many twentieth-century libertarians. Slavery is by definition the destruction of liberty and self-ownership.

Complicating the libertarian picture of the Civil War, however, is the fact that *warfare* is also destructive of liberty. In addition, allowing the *central* government to dominate subsidiary governments, such as those of the individual states, often reduces freedom.

Then again, *all* governments—including smaller local ones—are morally suspect according to libertarian thinking. Criticism of President Lincoln's suspension of civil liberties or his conduct of the Civil War should never be taken to vindicate slave owners. Nor should the condemnation of slavery be taken to excuse all actions taken by the Northern government, including the military draft, itself a form of slavery by libertarian standards.

While most libertarians agree that bundling historical and moral issues in this manner should be approached cautiously, lingering regional and ethnic tensions in the United States have sometimes been reflected in bitter arguments within today's libertarian movement over one or another faction's choice of emphasis in analyzing the Civil War. We will revisit those factions shortly.

THE ANARCHIST MOVEMENT
....

Almost as complex as the Civil War, though far less significant historically, was the American anarchist movement of the nineteenth century. For twenty-first century readers accustomed to the right-vs.-left model of politics, the nineteenth century might now appear a strange menagerie of mixed political elements, even beyond the anarchists.

Some of the most anti-government movements at the time were also anti-capitalist. Some of the most devoutly Christian communes also believed in free love, the abolition of marriage, and veganism. In a fashion similar to the New Age movement of the late twentieth century, faddish advocates of science and technology were also sometimes zealous mystics who believed that reality can be altered by a sufficiently powerful will. (This Transcendentalism-influenced idea continues to echo in the twenty-first century in the form of the Christian Science religion, various self-help movements, and the *Matrix* movies; via Ralph Waldo Emerson, it was also an influence on the German philosopher of "will," Friedrich Nietzsche.)

Aside from slavery, the most divisive American political issue of the nineteenth century may well have been *central banks*. (This was topical again after the Financial

Crisis that began in 2008, but for decades prior to that it was rarely a clear ideological dividing line in public debate, save in the rhetoric of certain libertarians.)

In that mixed political milieu, nineteenth-century anarchists ran the gamut from Marxists, who used the words anarchism and socialism almost interchangeably, to "individualist anarchists," who were often staunch advocates of property and trade. It is surprising in retrospect how long anarchism managed to endure as a coalition of what

now seem like divergent leftist and libertarian ideas. As late as the early twentieth century, individualist anarchist **Voltairine de Cleyre** and anti-capitalist anarchist **Emma Goldman** thought of themselves as allies, though the latter would briefly support the Bolshevik Revolution (before turning against it and nonetheless being deported back to Russia by American authorities).

> IN DEBATES BETWEEN ANARCHISTS AND STATISTS, THE BURDEN OF PROOF CLEARLY SHOULD REST ON THOSE WHO PLACE THEIR TRUST IN THE STATE. ANARCHY'S MAYHEM IS WHOLLY CONJECTURAL; THE STATE'S MAYHEM IS UNDENIABLY, FACTUALLY HORRENDOUS.

Robert Higgs, author of *Crisis and Leviathan* and senior fellow at the Independent Institute

One notion common among the left-anarchists of the nineteenth century—which kept them from worrying that the destruction of the state would be followed by a vicious battle between themselves and capitalistic individualist anarchists—was the idea that property and markets were themselves artificial constructs that would be unsustainable once the state was gone. Then again, even many hardcore Marxists of the day still believed in the withering away of the state and the spontaneous communes that would

arise in the state's absence. All the radicals seemed, for several decades, to be united in their opposition to existing states without yet worrying that the radicals themselves would be sharply divided once the state was gone.

It is easy for the twenty-first-century mind to forget how novel some of these ideas still were in the nineteenth century and how little time there had been to work out all the details and implications.

HENRY GEORGE AND THE ISSUE
OF LAND OWNERSHIP

Hard as it may be to imagine now, Americans at the start of the nineteenth century were still divided about the Lockean question of how much interaction with newly settled land was required before one could be said to own it. Did it merely have to be claimed? How much could be claimed? Did it have to be farmed? Did the vaguer, traditional boundaries of the Native Americans count? Should the government retain possession of large tracts of land? (It certainly has done so, with about a third of the land in the United States belonging to the government even today.)

The late nineteenth-century American economist Henry George, who was a libertarian in many respects, even made the argument—which might have resonated even more powerfully in places such as Europe or Latin America, full of landed gentry, than it did in the United States, the land of individual homesteaders—that ownership of a tract of land is not morally or legally legitimate in the way that ownership of smaller, transportable possessions is. Land ownership, George argued, unfairly favors whoever happened to get there first, including the descendants of long lines of aristocrats; that gave them vast unearned income from rents, as opposed to production.

The animosity toward *landlords* found in the writings of even more individualist and market-leaning anarchists of the nineteenth century fits well with the Georgist view

of land. Landlords are either the ultimate capitalists or
the least capitalist among us, depending on one's view of
land ownership. George's relatively moderate solution to
the pervasive problem was a "single tax" on land, with all
other taxes and economic regulations being abolished. In
other words, he called for a largely free market, except in
land. By that standard, one could argue that Hong Kong
in the late twentieth century—a largely unregulated and
free market but with all land technically owned by the government—was close to a Georgist paradise.

5 MODERN LIBERTARIANISM

IF THE UNITED STATES WAS divided about basic economics and banking, the nature of economics was becoming much clearer in the minds of others by the late nineteenth century. Notable among them was the Austrian school of economists. Before their rise to prominence, Central Europe had been influenced by pro-laissez faire, classical liberal philosophers such as **WILHELM VON HUMBOLDT**. By the 1880s, though, the authoritarian-conservative Prussian leader Otto von Bismarck was creating what was arguably the first modern welfare state. His explicit purpose was to make the populace more dependent on the government, undoing the nineteenth-century laissez-faire consensus.

THE AUSTRIAN SCHOOL

The early Austrian School economists do not sound like anti-statist ideologues by modern libertarian standards.

Several worked in government and saw themselves as advisers to the Austrian state, helping to prevent it making inefficient decisions (like some of the ones Bismarck was making over in Prussia). Vienna-based economists such as Eugen Böhm von Bawerk, Carl Menger, and Friedrich von Wieser also saw themselves as opponents of the Prussian Historical School of thought. Roughly speaking, the historicists, somewhat like Marx's philosophical forebear Georg Wilhelm Friedrich Hegel, tended to believe that the growth of the state—and specifically the unification of Germany—was a kind of historical destiny and that economic policy could be subordinated to political expediency without violating any vital, timeless laws of economics.

The Austrian School economists, by contrast, were adherents of *methodological individualism*. Sweeping aside ideas like nationalism, community, metaphysical duty, collective destiny, and historical dialectics, the Austrians recognized that subjective valuations by individuals (as described in Chapter 3) were the key to economic worth. Only by protecting individuals' property rights and letting them trade freely can we say with any confidence that they are being made happier, never in the end presuming to read their minds. Implicit in the Austrian School arguments, though not forcefully stated in the early years, was the idea that the emperor could not decide what was best for Austrian consumers any more than Otto von Bismarck could decide what was best for the Prussians who had so recently defeated the Austrians in war.

The two most famous early- and mid-twentieth-century exemplars of the Austrian view, which by then was losing out in the political realm to the advance of more statist economic thinking such as that of John Maynard Keynes, were **LUDWIG VON MISES** and **FRIEDRICH HAYEK,** one of several libertarians to win the Nobel Prize in economics.

> IF HISTORY COULD TEACH US ANYTHING,
> IT WOULD BE THAT PRIVATE PROPERTY IS
> INEXTRICABLY LINKED WITH CIVILIZATION.

LUDWIG VON MISES, *HUMAN ACTION*

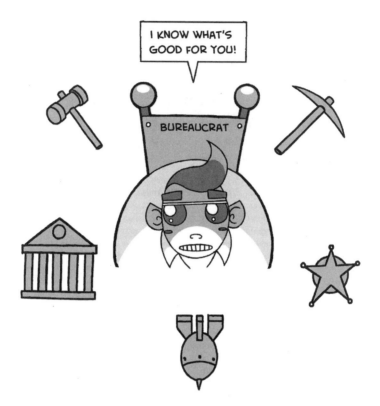

Mises' books communicate foundational Austrian principles with great clarity even for the layman. His masterpiece, *Human Action* (1949), starts from the simple premise that humans act and that we therefore know they have desires. The thwarting of those desires, whether through the sporadic property rights violations committed by common criminals or the systematic property rights violations committed by states, is a tragedy to be avoided. Although Mises was not an anarchist, some influenced by him would go on to see anarchism as the logical fulfill-ment of his ideas: all state action distorts human action and diverts human intentions away from their intended aims, misallocating resources.

Indeed, without the price signals generated by the mar-ket, there can be no meaningful way of knowing how to distribute resources. Do people want more chairs or more subtle shades of paint? Or both? And how much? Only the market can reveal the answers.

Hayek watered down some of Mises' insights while expanding upon others. Rather than emphasizing the meaninglessness of prices set without subjective individual valuations in the market, Hayek emphasized the fact that economic knowledge cannot easily be *centralized*, mak-ing the task of the central planner very difficult.

Economic knowledge is often local. The store owner knows when his goods have not sold and that knowledge helps him decide when to lower his price in the future. Millions of such decisions are made every day, and there is little hope that even the most well-meaning government can effectively replicate all of those decisions. For central planners to attempt to make an entire society's decisions is to set it on *The Road to Serfdom*, the title of Hayek's most popular work (1944). More a condemnation of World War II-era totalitarianism than of all government, *The Road to Serfdom* contains useful general libertarian arguments nonetheless.

Hayek went on to expand Austrian thinking into areas

Biography:
LUDWIG VON MISES (1881–1973)

Born in the Austo-Hungarian Empire in what

is now Ukraine, Mises came from a noble family of business-men, engineers, and mathematicians. He got a law degree and lectured on economics, heavily influenced by the work of founding Austrian economist Carl Menger and the lec-tures of Austrian economist Eugen Böhm von Bawerk. He fought in World War I and served as an economic advisor to the Austrian Chamber of Commerce and Austrian poli-ticians of both a fascistic and social-democratic bent. He left Austria in his thirties for Switzerland, married, and left Europe altogether in 1940 as the Nazis advanced across Europe, settling in the United States.

Mises received grants from the Rockefeller University and Volker Fund as well as one of the trustees of New York University, where he was a visiting professor and a great influence on Murray Rothbard and other New York libertarians, including Ayn Rand. With Friedrich Hayek, Milton Friedman, and other prominent libertarians, Mises co-founded the free-market Mont Pelerin Society in 1947 in hopes of restoring the lost classical liberal social order in the wake of World War II.

Mises sought to explain all of free-market economics as a logical deduction from a few undeniable observations about reality. The first of these is the fact that "humans act," the starting point of his 1949 masterpiece, *Human Action*.

Economics should not be just the accumulation of statistics or other data in the absence of an explanatory theory, he believed, but rather a science of the logically necessary consequences of human action, or **praxeology**.

Human Action was in a sense the positive version of the negative consequences of intervention and interference in markets that Mises described in his early work, *Socialism* (1922). Between these extremes, he described broader, intermediary political principles in short popularizations such as *Liberalism* (1927), in which he defended the classical, pre-twentieth-century conception of that philosophy (and earned undue criticism decades later for a brief, passing reference to the fledgling fascist movement as a possible counterweight to Communism).

During World War II, Mises published increasingly dire analyses of the effects of totalitarian planning, in works such as *Interventionism* (1941), *Omnipotent Government* (1944), and *Bureaucracy* (1944), followed after the war by *Planned Chaos* (1947).

In an age when most intellectuals believed socialism (in some form) was the essence of rational planning, Mises tirelessly made the case that, in the absence of the price signals created by free trade in all goods among willing buyers and sellers, "prices" and the decisions about how to set them and how to allocate goods will be meaningless, leading inevitably to shortages and other economic disruptions. This was considered a key contribution to the ongoing argument in the early twentieth century often referred to as the "socialist calculation debate."

of social analysis not normally touched upon by economists. He observed, for example, that institutions and traditions (such as language) evolve over time in a weeding-out process similar to the fading away of uncompetitive business models. This evolutionary view was similar to that expressed by late-nineteenth-century English philoso-

pher and scientist **HERBERT SPENCER**, who coined the phrase "survival of the fittest" even before Darwin popularized the idea of natural selection in biology. Neither Spencer nor Hayek wanted the poor or the weak to suffer, as some have glibly alleged. Rather, they observed that practices (particularly violence) that increase poverty tend to become less popular over the long haul and that practices (particularly nonviolence) that lead to prosperity become more popular.

In Hayek's case, that hope is simultaneously a vindication of progress *and* of enduring traditions, which compelled him to write an essay explaining "Why I Am Not a Conservative." He nonetheless remains one of conser-

Biography:

FRIEDRICH HAYEK (1899-1992)

Born in Vienna and, like his economic

mentor Mises, serving in World War I, Hayek was eager to see humanity avoid repeating the statist disasters of that conflict, including communist revolution and the kind of economic planning that was routine under wartime regimentation. Hayek moved to England just prior to World War II and went on to teach at the London School of Economics, the University of Chicago, and the University of Freiburg. Unlike Mises, he was eventually a recipient of the Nobel Prize for Economics (1974) as well as the Presidential Medal of Freedom (1991) and many other honors. His layman-friendly anti-totalitarian book *The Road to Serfdom* (1944) remained for decades after its publication one of the most widely read libertarian or conservative volumes ever written.

In much the same way that Adam Smith described "the Invisible Hand," Edmund Burke described tradition, and Herbert Spencer described the "survival of the fittest" as unplanned competitive mechanisms by which the best practices tend to win out over unsustainable ones, so Hayek came to see society as a "spontaneous order"—from everyday economic decision-making to the evolution of language—that no central planner could hope to replicate in all its subtlety. Attempting to do so, he maintained, would lead only to a tragically inefficient approximation of a functioning society.

Hayek retained some sympathy for the aspirations of "the socialists of all parties," as he put it in the dedication to *Road to Serfdom*, seeing the temptation to central planning as something to which all factions are susceptible. According to some of his more radical libertarian critics, however, he retained entirely too much sympathy for socialism, along with a long list of useful functions he thought government might plausibly serve, so long as they do not lead to true central planning.

In works such as *The Counter-Revolution of Science* (1952), Hayek harshly condemned the "scientistic" belief in technocratic social engineering, seeing it as the misapplication of ideas that worked well in engineering and other hard sciences. He warned against the constructivist rationalism (akin to the world-remaking ambition of the French Revolutionaries or Bolsheviks) that leads people to believe they can draw up a blueprint for rebuilding the world from scratch. He described a more positive yet humble vision of economic and legal institutions evolving in beneficial fashion over time in works such as *The Constitution of Liberty* (1960) and *Law, Legislation, and Liberty* (3 vols., 1973–1979).

vatives' favorite libertarians—and a favorite of leftists as well, since he casually accepted a rather long list of legitimate functions of government (from unemployment

insurance to weights and measures). In his later writings, Hayek seemed to accept the idea that government itself might evolve as part of the "spontaneous order" of a free and liberal society (the opposite of a single, dictatorial blueprint imposed from the center). For good or ill, even leftists such as Ralph Nader have praised Hayek.

BOOMS AND BUSTS

Another Austrian view that has gained widespread mainstream attention is the **AUSTRIAN VIEW OF THE "BUSINESS CYCLE,"** or periodic economic booms and busts. The Austrian School suggests that this pattern, rather than being just a natural side effect of markets, may be fueled in part by the continual printing of new units of government-made currency by central banks. The underlying theory of the proponents of central banking is that stimulating business activity is inherently good and that central banks can do so by creating the false impression that, since prices rise as units of currency increase, actual wealth and returns on investments must be increasing as well. In truth, the Austrians would argue, if the increase in prices (inflation) is largely illusory—if the same amount of wealth is merely denoted by a larger number of bills—the overinvestment or malinvestment will eventually be recognized, and stocks will experience a harsh correction.

Fear of such a correction was a major source of debate among economists during the Great Depression and among critics of the easy-money policies, or "quantitative easing" (combined with "stimulus spending"), of central banks following the 2008 financial crisis.

MARXISM, PROGRESSIVISM, AND CENTRAL PLANNING

Unfortunately from a libertarian perspective, by the time of the Great Depression, Western civilization already had lost much of its earlier enthusiasm for markets. Despite creating unprecedented growth and well-being—roughly doubling human lifespans and tripling the population of Europe over the course of the nineteenth century—capitalism had come to be seen by many as a disruptive, blind, cruel force that replaced idyllic farm life with the harsh factory conditions of the Industrial Revolution. Intellectuals revolted and harbored dreams of designing a better, kinder society.

Almost immediately after the death of the great anti-capitalist philosopher Karl Marx in 1883, intellectuals

in England created the Fabian Society, aimed at slowly, stealthily turning society socialist. (This actually ran counter to the revolutionary methods Marx described, which would be echoed in the 1917 Bolshevik Revolution in Russia, albeit in a more agrarian society than Marx expected.) Meanwhile, in the United States, works such as the 1888 novel *Looking Backward: 2000-1887* by Edward Bellamy envisioned a future of rational centralized planning instead of competition and capitalism. (His cousin, Francis Bellamy, was both a socialist and a minister who wrote the Pledge of Allegiance with the conscious aim of inspiring cult-like allegiance to the state; ironically, conservatives would go on to be the Pledge's most ardent defenders.) Bellamy's book became one of the most popular ever published in the United States, helping to inspire Progressivism, a movement comparable to England's Fabian Socialism in its gradualism.

Progressivism, too, would focus on piecemeal reforms, but it also emphasized a partnership between the centralized state and large, centralized industrial corporations. Both the Republican president Teddy Roosevelt and the Democratic president Woodrow Wilson paid homage to Progressivism, seeing themselves as opponents both of the old laissez-faire constitutional order and of socialist radicalism. The result was that, despite the depiction of big business and big government as foes in the rhetoric of many right- and left-leaning intellectuals, in practice, thanks to ever more elaborate regulations and subsidies, they were now deeply entwined partners.

The partnership was sealed with the creation, in 1913, of the Federal Reserve, the United States' central bank and an increasingly influential driver of business cycles and monetary policy. In theory, the Federal Reserve would smooth out the business cycle. In practice, it was on the job only 16 years before the greatest depression of all time. And, in truth, though Western societies since the early twentieth century have not been truly socialist, neither have they been laissez-faire, instead opting for variations of a "mixed economy," more corporatist and welfare-statist than either wholly free-market or wholly planned.

Even among leftists, the new emphasis on central planning caused something of a rift. In New York City in the early twentieth century, there were divisive arguments between, on one hand, Greenwich Village radicals who favored bohemian lifestyles and opposed World War I (such as Randolph Bourne, whose posthumous 1918 manuscript *The State* warned that "War is the health of the state") and, on the other hand, the Progressives, centered on such outlets as *The New Republic* magazine, which favored centralized planning, Wilsonian wars-for-democracy, and the homogenization of immigrant populations. Some Progressives, of course, were also advocates of explicitly racist eugenics, alcohol prohibition, and the institution of minimum wage laws as a deliberate means of eliminating low-wage jobs and driving poor immigrant workers back to their home countries.

Progressive policies would endure to our own day in some cases, albeit with superficially different rationales in

keeping with changing social mores. Only after the wide-spread acceptance of certain aesthetic and behavioral elements of hippie culture six decades later, and shortly after bitter leftist infighting over the Vietnam War, would the left really overcome its rift between the central planners and the bohemians.

Long before that, President Calvin Coolidge was perhaps the last gasp of the old laissez-faire thinking in the Oval Office and a disillusioned Progressive who had concluded that government was usually best off doing nothing. Or as he put it, "the chief business of the American people is business." Still, Coolidge is remembered now as much for the Depression that came after his presidency as for the immense prosperity that occurred during it. Ideologically, it was the Depression-driven statism of President Franklin Roosevelt that ended up dominating U.S. thinking for generations to come.

Roosevelt was not without strong critics. Many on what is now termed **"THE OLD RIGHT,"** such as Albert Jay Nock and H.L. Mencken, were largely libertarian in their denunciations of FDR and his plans for the regimentation of American society. Mencken's biting humor, directed at government and religion alike, was heavily influenced by the radicalism of Friedrich Nietzsche. Of the state's parasitism and politicians' promises, he wrote, "Every election is a sort of advance auction sale of stolen goods."

Faced with the rise of totalitarianism in Germany, Russia, and China—and the decline of old, classical liberalism in Western nations—Hayek and Mises, who had fled Continental Europe and the Nazis, nearly despaired of liberty ever being restored. After the war, though, Hayek and others founded the **MONT PELERIN SOCIETY**, which began meeting in Switzerland in 1947 to discuss how to restore classical liberal values. What would later come to be called "libertarianism" was by then sharpening into a more precise ideology. Mises famously condemned even the very laissez-faire Mont Pelerin Society participants for straying from free-market orthodoxy, telling them at the first meeting, "You're all a bunch of socialists."

MILTON FRIEDMAN AND THE CHICAGO SCHOOL

That was the recollection of Nobel Prize-winning libertarian economist Milton Friedman, who would himself go on to become one of the most influential and popular advo-

cates of the libertarian position, advising presidents and tirelessly using op-eds and TV appearances to dissect pro-government arguments. Friedman's more mathematical and historical approach to economic analysis is often seen as the feature that distinguished the Chicago School of economics (centered originally on the University of Chicago) from the deductive Austrian School. Friedman is sometimes credited with convincing President Richard Nixon to end the military draft. Yet he is also criticized by more radical libertarians for helping to persuade Nixon and many American conservatives that it would be safe to go off the

gold standard in the 1970s, so long as government continued to print currency at a steady and predictable rate. Unfortunately, the temptation is immense for any government central bank to engage in inflation and try to time an economic boom for political effect.

For sounding mildly sympathetic to rent control, Friedman was even condemned as a "red" in a letter written by novelist and philosopher Ayn Rand to the **FOUNDATION FOR ECONOMIC EDUCATION**. (FEE, the first libertarian think tank, was founded by Leonard Read in 1946. Read also wrote the essay "I, Pencil," popularized by Friedman, to explain how markets coordinate radically decentralized production processes, such as the making of a pencil, that no one person is likely to understand in their entirety.)

As what would soon be dubbed "libertarianism" sharpened into a coherent ideology, it also gained increasingly clear and ardent polemicists. A quartet of female writers around World War II, often credited with helping to bring libertarian thinking to the masses, included **ROSE WILDER LANE** (ghostwriter of her mother Laura Ingalls Wilder's *Little House on the Prairie* books and author in her own right of the libertarian manifesto *The Discovery of Freedom*); **ISABEL PATERSON** (whose manifesto *God of the Machine* depicted freedom as a sort of spiritual force that should not be stymied); **ZORA NEALE HURSTON** (whose novels depicted firsthand the hardships of the American black experience while valorizing self-help and freedom rather than statist solutions); and Rand.

AYN RAND AND OBJECTIVISM

Ayn Rand fled Soviet Russia and lived in Hollywood for a time, writing now-obscure screenplays, Nietzsche-influenced plays, and unpublished novels. With the success of her 1943 novel *The Fountainhead* about an architect with uncompromising intellectual integrity, she began developing a philosophy of her own. Her system of ideas was fully libertarian but included other elements as well, addressing everything from aesthetics and psychology to metaphysics. Although most libertarians would say that one can be a philosophically consistent libertarian without

Biography:
MILTON FRIEDMAN (1912-2006)

One of the most influential economists of the twentieth century, Friedman was born in New York City but is most closely associated with the University of Chicago, where he taught for more than 30 years and was part of the so-called Chicago School of economists.

Friedman was best known to the general public as a tireless defender, in books, columns, TV interviews, and his PBS series **Free to Choose**, of laissez-faire capitalism and libertarianism, explaining the basics of free markets and property rights in a combative yet endlessly cheerful fashion. He was an influence on the free-market views of the Reagan administration and various circles of the conservative establishment in the United States and around the world.

During the Nixon administration, Friedman served on a federal commission examining the prospects for an all-volunteer military, which contributed greatly to the abandonment of conscription in 1973. He was also a major influence on the rise of the school choice movement and contributed to greater acceptance on the political right of the idea of drug legalization. Friedman's more radical libertarian critics have faulted him for his small wartime role in administering withholding taxes and his later pivotal role in persuading the Nixon administration that it would be safe to abandon the gold standard.

As a founder of "monetarism," Friedman was aware of the dangers of inflation and technically opposed the existence of the Federal Reserve. But so long as a central bank exists, he maintained, it can stimulate aggregate demand, and thus economic productivity, through careful, predictable expansion of the currency supply. (In practice, as libertarians often lament, currency-printing is timed for political effect, contributing to booms and busts and making it more difficult for businesses to make long-term price calculations.) Friedman's book *A Monetary History of the United States, 1867–1960,* co-written with Anna Schwartz, blamed the Great Depression in part on the Federal Reserve reducing its currency-printing *too soon* during the initial crisis.

Even if there are traces of John Maynard Keynes's thinking in his macroeconomic views, Friedman's clear exposition of the basics of microeconomic and free-market thinking in layman-friendly books such as *Capitalism and Freedom* (1962) and *Free to Choose* (co-written with wife Rose Friedman, 1980) have made him one of the most effective communicators of capitalist ideas in all of history.

The Friedman family seems to have become more radical with each generation, with Milton's son, law professor David D. Friedman, espousing anarcho-capitalism, the complete elimination of government, and David's son Patri Friedman abandoning altogether the hope of reforming or eliminating existing, land-based governments (instead urging the creation of new governments based on floating platforms in the ocean, so-called "seasteading").

sharing (or even being aware of) all of Rand's views, she did not see it that way. Notoriously rigid in her thinking, she condemned as irrational those who were acquainted with but refused to adopt her philosophy, which she called **OBJECTIVISM**.

"MY DEAR FELLOW, WHO WILL LET YOU?"
"THAT'S NOT THE POINT. THE POINT
IS, WHO WILL STOP ME?"

FROM *THE FOUNTAINHEAD* **BY AYN RAND**

No doubt reacting strongly against the collectivism of her native Russia—where she had seen her family's property confiscated by the state—Rand rejected not just totalitarianism and big government but the collectivist attitudes that made them possible. She went so far as to condemn altruism (properly defined) as an impediment to self-interested individual flourishing. Just as she remade herself in Hollywood, Rand believed that all people should be free to live their own lives, for themselves, not feeling duty-bound to sacrifice themselves for others. She saw the same basic impulse to self-sacrifice in both statism and religion, which claim to protect people but end by destroying them for the sake of a purportedly "larger" ideal.

Her mammoth 1957 novel *Atlas Shrugged* unveils Rand's philosophy in full while depicting the collapse of a near-future United States into dysfunctional crony capitalism and socialism. Despite the claims by critics that

Rand viewed the poor with contempt and lionized all successful businesspeople, nearly all the many villains in the novel are businessmen who eschew strict adherence to property rights in favor of bailouts and regulatory protections from the government. They drive the economy into the ground while paying occasional lip service to

Biography:
AYN RAND (1905–1982)

Alisa Zinov'yevna Rosenbaum was born in St. Petersburg, later called Petrograd, and developed an interest in writing novels and plays at an early age. Her father was a pharmacist and landlord whose property was seized during Russia's October 1917 Bolshevik Revolution, though the family had been sympathetic to the short-lived moderate socialist government that existed between the March overthrow of Czar Nicholas II and the seizure of power by Lenin's Bolsheviks.

After four years in Crimea, then dominated by the doomed anti-Communist White Russian army, the family returned to Petrograd and experienced extreme poverty. To the atheist views of Rand's teenage years were added a fierce hatred of the Communists. While studying at Petrograd University (before being expelled for being part of the bourgeoisie), her early philosophical thinking was particularly influenced by Aristotle and Nietzsche.

Using a travel visa to visit Chicago relatives in 1926, Rand decided never to return to her native Russia. Instead, she traveled on to Hollywood, where she worked as a film extra, assistant screenwriter, and soon writer of minor screenplays. She married fledgling actor Frank O'Connor in 1929 and urged her relatives in Russia to join her; they were never permitted to leave Russia.

Drawing upon her love of Romantic authors such as Victor Hugo, she began writing novels, at first unpublished, and plays. Her first stage drama to be produced, *The Night of January 16th*, later a film, was perhaps the most overtly Nietzschean of her early works. The play invited a jury made up of actual audience members to judge a character who might have broken laws, possibly even committed murder, to rescue a business. The play differs subtly from her later work in asking the audience to sympathize with the central characters more because of their determination and strength than because of their adherence to property rights and honesty per se.

Rand went from favoring Franklin Roosevelt for his opposition to Prohibition to detesting him for his regulation of business. Although she hated totalitarianism, as evidenced by her novel about Russia, *We the Living* (1935), and her science fiction novella *Anthem* (1938), it was with her 1943 novel *The Fountainhead*, about an individualistic architect named Howard Roark, that she most clearly began advancing a philosophy fully integrating her individualistic take on psychology with laissez-faire capitalism and an aversion to the self-sacrificing ethos of social workers and leftist intellectuals.

Through her best-selling 1957 novel *Atlas Shrugged*, numerous public appearances and interviews, and her organization's newsletters, Rand spread her fully developed philosophy, called Objectivism because it rejected moral and epistemological relativism, to millions. Even after her death in 1982, the Ayn Rand Institute, her former lover Nathaniel Branden, a slightly more moderate breakaway group called the Objectivist Center, and numerous other organizations and individuals influenced by her philosophy continued to spread and debate her ideas — from the philosopher Tibor Machan to the comic book character Mr. A, created by original Spider-Man artist Steve Ditko.

Atlas Shrugged has remained one of the best-selling novels of all time, seeing upticks in sales when Communism collapsed circa 1989 and again when crony capitalism contracted in the financial crisis of 2008. Condemnations of her work in left-leaning publications were almost nonstop thereafter, but her influence continued to spread.

productivity and entrepreneurship, mixed with altruistic slogans about equality and rescuing the masses.

The real victims in *Atlas Shrugged* are not the persecuted laissez-faire holdouts among the tycoons so much as the masses of ordinary citizens who lack the philosophical foundations that would enable them to see that a bogus, sacrifice-based morality and an illegitimate, enslaving government have been imposed upon them. To guilt-trip people into compliance, Rand warns, makes them silent and more easily governed. Since the police cannot be everywhere at all times to enforce rules directly, every oppressive system seeks to gain "the sanction of the victim."

Just as *Fountainhead* praised artistic integrity, so *Atlas* celebrates intellectual integrity on multiple fronts, its villains routinely engaging in intellectual evasions and verbal dodges to maintain their belief, or apparent belief, in a doomed system that they cannot confront honestly. The one man with the courage to condemn the very foundations of the faltering society, John Galt, caps his rebellion not with a massive armed assault but with a lengthy radio address that explains the philosophical errors of the regime. The conflicted main characters of the novel are industrialists such as railroad magnate Dagny Taggart who have not yet summoned the courage to admit that the existing altruist, socialist, mystical social order cannot be saved and must be allowed to collapse before humanity can rebuild.

Rand amassed a huge following, and Objectivists continue to form a substantial subset of libertarians even while operating as a movement unto themselves. During Rand's lifetime, the movement was centered on her beloved eventual home city, New York. Her organization, run for a time by the self-help-oriented psychotherapist **NATHANIEL BRANDEN**, was headquartered for years on the first floor of the Empire State Building. She introduced millions of people to free-market arguments but also provided critics of laissez-faire with numerous additional targets, from her atheism to her unabashed belief in, as one collection of her essays puts it, *The Virtue of Selfishness*.

MURRAY ROTHBARD

One New Yorker who wearied of Rand's cult-leader tendencies but rose to comparable influence in the movement himself was NYU-based economist and economic historian Murray Rothbard. (He left Rand's circle after she tried to badger Rothbard's wife into renouncing her belief in God.) Rothbard, who showed dashes of the Old Right's thinking, got his start in politics campaigning for free-market anti-militarist and FDR foe Senator Robert A. Taft for president (even though Taft was considered too sympathetic to the New Deal by some in the Republican Party). Rothbard's career was characterized by shifting political allegiances and movements back and forth across the political spectrum in search of allies and enemies.

TAXATION IS THEFT, PURELY AND SIMPLY, EVEN THOUGH IT IS THEFT ON A GRAND AND COLOSSAL SCALE WHICH NO ACKNOWLEDGED CRIMINALS COULD HOPE TO MATCH. IT IS A COMPULSORY SEIZURE OF THE PROPERTY OF THE STATE'S INHABITANTS, OR SUBJECTS.

MURRAY ROTHBARD, *THE ETHICS OF LIBERTY*

In economics, he was an Austrian and became the greatest proselytizer for Mises' views. It was Rothbard who decisively wedded the old word "libertarianism" to the specific creed that denounces property rights violations and depicts government as a systematic, chronic violation of property rights. He did not exactly create the philosophy but did a great deal to create the libertarian movement as it now exists, beginning in the mid-1960s. He broke with the mainstream right over the military draft and was mischievously contrarian in defending such actions as Latin American revolutionary land-grabs that could be, but rarely were, defended on libertarian grounds. (In the Latin American example, radical opposition groups retook property seized by force generations earlier or protected by kleptocratic regimes that suppressed commerce and kept people poor.) Unfailingly antiwar, he even strayed at times (a bit like Noam Chomsky) into reflexive defense of U.S. enemies, including the North Vietnamese communists, against U.S. imperialism.

Rothbard's associate **KARL HESS** is the only person ever to co-write speeches for Barry Goldwater (including, it is believed, Goldwater's speech defending "extremism in the defense of liberty") and also to become an associate and defender of the Black Panthers (who advocated **GUN OWNERSHIP** and self-help in addition to their black militancy).

In his economic theory, Rothbard came close to overcoming the oft-noted clash between *rights*-oriented thinking and *utilitarian* thinking. If the subjectivist Austrian view is correct, after all, every violation of property rights risks decreasing human happiness. Such violations at the very least take us from the realm of revealed preferences

Biography:
MURRAY ROTHBARD (1926–1995)

The Manhattan-dwelling son of Eastern European

immigrant Jewish parents, Murray Rothbard was sympathetic to libertarian-leaning "Old Right" writers such as essayist H.L. Mencken and novelist Garett Garrett prior to World War II. During the war he attended Columbia University, acquiring a mathematics undergraduate degree and a decade later an economics Ph.D. from the same institution.

In his 1962 book *Man, Economy, and State*, Rothbard explained and expanded upon the work of economist Ludwig von Mises, hewing to the latter's Austrian School view of methodological individualism and *praxeology* (the literal "science of action," or the deduced necessary consequences of human action, regardless of political or philosophical hopes to the contrary — economic laws without apologies, evasions, or mountains of statistics and graphs).

For Rothbard, supply and demand, mutually beneficial exchange, and competition for greater market share through reduced prices and/or increased quality were not just statistical trends but basic, near-universal principles of life.

With his wife, JoAnn Schumacher (1928–1999), Rothbard acquired a circle of intellectual friends, initially based in New York City, where he wrote for the free-market Volker Fund and taught at Brooklyn Polytechnic Institute. He later taught at University of Nevada, Las Vegas, where he was a great influence on the philosopher Hans-Hermann Hoppe. For a time during his New York years, Rothbard also participated in Ayn Rand's discussion circle before growing disillusioned with her.

Rothbard's activities outside academia were arguably just as important as his voluminous academic writings and his popularizations. Inspired in part by such nineteenth-century individualist anarchists as Lysander Spooner and Benjamin Tucker, he moved beyond his right-wing roots to seek an alliance with the late-1960s left amid the revolutionary fervor of groups such as the Students for a Democratic Society (SDS) and the editors of *Ramparts* magazine.

It was in part by allying with other disaffected Republicans, however, that he co-founded the Libertarian Party in the 1970s and later the Cato Institute and Ludwig von Mises Institute.

His views shifted in his final years back toward the right, albeit with a dissident faction of conservatives — the paleoconservatives and paleolibertarians — who resented the mainstream right's embrace of the military-industrial complex, globalism, and mass immigration.

Though Rothbard's headquarters in his final, post-Cold War years was the Mises Institute — headed by writer/editor Lew Rockwell, sometimes criticized for "neo-Confederate," anti-Lincoln views — his skepticism about mass immigration was reportedly fueled less by racism than by observation of the consequences for satellite nations near Russia and China of mass immigration by communists. Rothbard feared that socialist immigrants, in a majoritarian democracy, tend to bring with them not merely a desire for welfare-state services but also a belief in even more socialist policies.

into the hopelessly ambiguous realm of attempting to esti-
mate other people's happiness. With the latter comes all
the potential for selfishness and abuse that provides the
party doing the evaluating—who is likely the party doing
the regulating and the redistributing.

By taking libertarian arguments to their logical conclusion and recommending that all governmental tasks
be privatized, including courts and defense, Rothbard
was the real creator of a distinct version of libertarianism
called **ANARCHO-CAPITALISM.** (We'll hear more
about that in Chapter 7.) As an economic historian, he
had the advantage of being able to point to real historical examples of seemingly essential government functions that were successfully privatized. In articles for the
magazine *Ramparts*, Rothbard and his associates, amid
the political tumult of the late 1960s, attempted to create
a radical libertarian-left coalition to replace the libertar-
ian-right coalition he and his associates had abandoned
for the time being. Through it all, Rothbard, even as an
anarchist, continued to defend the practice of voting (as
an act of self-defense) and to pick favored and disfavored
candidates on the mainstream political scene.

By all accounts a "happy warrior," Rothbard never trans-
lated his anarchism into a sullen detachment from society.
He experimented with many different avenues of political
engagement, and he casts a shadow throughout the rest
of our story, up to and beyond his death in 1995 at age 68.

VEHICLES AND INSTITUTIONS

Most libertarians are not as content to alienate people as the dogmatic Rand or schismatic Rothbard were. Libertarians have tried many avenues of outreach to spread the message to the rest of the public.

Reason magazine began publication in 1968 and grew from a low-budget, mimeographed newsletter to become the slick flagship magazine of the movement. Over the years, it gradually shifted in focus from ideological/philosophical to economic/analytical and then to hip/reportorial. Its affiliated think tank, the Reason Foundation, remained headquartered in Los Angeles while the magazine itself relocated to Washington, D.C. Engaging regularly with mainstream political pundits and journalists, the

SPACEX IS AN EXAMPLE OF AN ENTREPRENEURIAL MARKET-DRIVEN ALTERNATIVE TO BLOATED GOVERNMENT BUREAUCRACIES.

publication has been treated with respect even by many ideological foes in the twenty-first century. By contrast, **Liberty** maga-zine (the one long edited by R.W. Bradford, not other publications by the same name) was aimed more at an internal libertarian-movement audi-ence after its founding in 1987.

The **LIBERTARIAN PARTY** was founded in 1971 in the Colorado home of David F. Nolan. Rothbard was among the party's earliest featured participants, though he soon grew disillusioned with it. The LP, as it is often called, is arguably the most successful third party in post-war American history (though that isn't saying much in America's two-party-dominated system). Notable figures who have run on the LP presidential ticket include Tonie Nathan, who as the LP's vice presidential candidate in 1972 became the first female or Jewish candidate to win an electoral vote; David Koch (one of the two politically active billionaire Koch Brothers who became frequent targets of the left in the early twenty-first century) as

the vice-presidential candidate in 1980; occasional Repub-lican congressman Ron Paul of Texas, the LP's choice for president in 1988; former Republican congressman Bob Barr of Georgia, the presidential nominee in 2008; and former Republican governor of New Mexico Gary John-son, who headed the ticked in 2012.

The LP has occasionally gotten members elected to local

office, but it has never managed to get more than about
1% of the vote in a presidential election (Ed Clark's run in
1980 and Gary Johnson's run in 2012), though they make
an effort every four years. Whether the LP is useful as an
awareness-raising vehicle or merely foolhardy is a topic
debated in the broader movement, not to mention among
Republicans who resent having a rival for the free-market vote. (They argue that splitting
that vote could empower Democrats.)
Some libertarians reject voting altogether, believing that it encourages
politicians and lulls the public into
believing government is responsive to their needs.

A MAN IS NO LESS A SLAVE BECAUSE
HE IS ALLOWED TO CHOOSE A NEW
MASTER ONCE IN A TERM OF YEARS.

LYSANDER SPOONER, "THE
CONSTITUTION OF NO AUTHORITY"

Nolan's awareness-raising accomplishments include
devising the so-called **NOLAN DIAMOND** as an
alternative model of political preferences to the standard
right-left "spectrum." The Diamond uses two axes, one for
"economic" and one for "personal" liberties, making it possible for someone who favors the libertarian view on both
to be placed at the apex; an authoritarian who believes in

government control in both spheres is placed at the bottom; someone who believes in complete personal liberty (legalized drugs and prostitution, say) but no economic liberty (favors complete socialist control of the economy) is placed at the far-left corner of the diamond, and someone who opposes personal liberty but favors economic liberty is placed at the far-right corner.

While even this model does not capture the full spectrum of ideological possibilities in a multivariable world, it's a big improvement. Literally, it helps put libertarians, who are "neither right nor left," on the map.

Some of those disillusioned with the LP's efforts in the 1970s left the party around 1980 to start think tanks, most of which are focused on giving advice to the more established political parties. Among the numerous libertarian think tanks operating today, two of the most prominent ones help define different factions of the movement: the **CATO INSTITUTE** and the slightly younger **LUDWIG VON MISES INSTITUTE** (named after the Austrian economist but not solely dedicated to spreading his work). Both were co-founded by Rothbard (along with one of the Koch Brothers in the case of Cato), though, as he was prone to do, he soon had a falling out with Cato.

The tension between the Cato Institute and the Mises Institute can be summed up in different ways. The former is located in Washington, D.C., the latter in Alabama; the former produces practical white papers that appeal to wonks of all ideological stripes, while the latter issues hardcore polemics that call for abolishing the dollar and eliminating the military-industrial complex. But another key difference is a phenomenon familiar to many movements, whether in politics, religion, or the arts: the tension between seeking mainstream acceptance for sometimes-

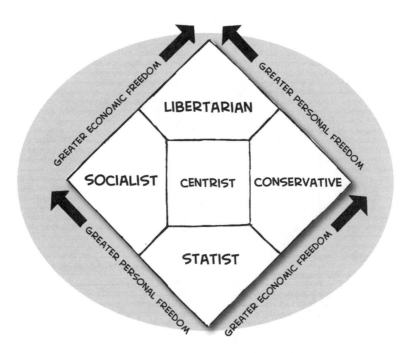

radical ideas (Cato) and condemning the mainstream with consistently radical ideas (Mises). Neither is the obvious winning strategy. Each has its pitfalls, as critics from the other camp allege.

Too much deference to mainstream sensibilities can lead to complacency—such as accepting the importance of set-

ting the D.C. policy agenda. Too much zealous detachment from the mainstream can lead to insularity, dogmatism, and susceptibility to crank views—such as belief in the advisability of reaching out to racists or militia men. Over time, however, libertarians in general have become more self-aware about their internal differences and about how they are perceived by society in general. As with so many things, libertarians hope that competition may yet bring out the best in all factions.

FUSIONISM

One important effort to boost mainstream acceptance of libertarian ideas during the Cold War was what *National Review* editor (and former communist) Frank Meyer called "fusionism." This is the somewhat Hayekian idea that tradition and markets naturally complement each other, since many moral practices, such as paying one's debts, help smooth commerce. Thus, Meyer believed that conservatism and libertarianism are natural allies, even elements of one larger philosophy. Seen in this way, not only the Cold War free-market Republican coalition but the earlier Victorian combination of moral rigidity and capitalism—and bourgeois society in general—look more natural. (Something like fusionism would be dubbed "Conservatarianism" in the 2010s by another *National Review* contributor, Charles C.W. Cooke.)

Perhaps, adherents of fusionism would argue, libertarianism is better thought of as a form of conservatism than as a curious right/left hybrid. However, critics allege that fusionism reduced libertarians to a mere constituency of the Republican Party, taken for granted the way Rea-

ganites assumed they could count on Friedmanites to be loyal coalition members. (Reaganites also thought they could count on them not to be too critical of conservative excesses, so long as they fit broadly into legitimate minarchist functions of the state, such as policing and national defense.) As is so often the case, there may be some truth in both the fusionists' and anti-fusionists' views.

THE CONTEMPORARY MOVEMENT

It was really with the end of the Cold War in 1989 that the contemporary libertarian milieu began to take shape. The 1990s were a time of great moderation in retrospect, with the sudden absence of the Soviet Union seeming to eliminate the longstanding need for ideological rigidity and with it the need for many longstanding coalitions. Increased peace and prosperity, combined with a new optimism about technology thanks to the spread of the Internet, seemed to provide breathing room in which Americans could experiment with some looser new political-philosophical ideas.

The 1990s saw the brief rise of "market socialism" as a proposed third-way replacement for European communism, the spread of communitarianism in the West, and the global ratcheting up of environmentalism. The libertarian movement drifted away from the Republican Party into both a sort of "lifestyle liberalism" and more obscure forms of conservatism. In very mainstream circles, the decade brought the renewed dominance of **NEOLIBERALISM**, a vague term essentially referring to twentieth-century welfare-state liberalism, newly tempered by a greater respect for the benefits of economic growth and global trade. This philosophy was well-suited to rationalizing the policy decisions of moderate-left politicians such as U.S. president Bill Clinton and British prime minister Tony Blair.

Meanwhile, the Republican Congress elected in 1994, after decades out of power, struck some libertarian themes about downsizing and decentralizing government. Most notable was the House Republicans' **"CONTRACT WITH AMERICA"** statement of principles. Although few reforms or budget cuts became law, even the ex-Communists of Mongolia looked to the Republican Congress for reform ideas.

In this moderate yet seemingly market-friendly environment, libertarian groups such as the **INSTITUTE FOR HUMANE STUDIES** focused on gentler outreach to academics and students sympathetic to free-market ideas who were not necessarily full-fledged libertarians. (Full disclosure: it was around this period that the author of the current volume became involved in the libertarian movement.)

Much of the post-Cold War political optimism, as well as the libertarian comfort with loosely defined ideological boundaries, would end with the terrorist attacks of Sept. 11, 2001.

TWENTY-FIRST-CENTURY FACTIONS

OT ONLY WAS THE LIBERTARIAN
movement no longer comfortably on the same page
as conservatives in a broader free-market coalition during and after the George W. Bush presidency (2001–2009),
but libertarianism's internal divisions were made deeper
by varying reactions to that rift, by both Bush's and Barack
Obama's handling of civil liberties, by the protracted financial crisis, and by social media fostering ever more finely
divided ideological micro-cultures, especially among mil-
lennials.

NEOLIBERTARIANISM

A few libertarians, reacting to the threat of Islamic terrorism, began using the term "neolibertarianism," in imitation
of the newly dominant strain of hawkish "neoconserva-
tism." Adding to the confusion of the political lexicon,
both of those terms had been used before with different

meanings. "Neolibertarians" were sometimes referenced in contrast to "geolibertarians," who shared the Georgist view of the morally dubious status of land ownership. "Neoconservatives" originally referred less to a foreign policy faction than to 1960s conservatives who had departed the left due to increasing disillusionment with the sociological side effects of the hippie-era counterculture. Military defense is seen as a legitimate function of the state by minarchists, but war should remain a last resort in the minds of most libertarians. The necessity of U.S. military intervention in Afghanistan, and even more so Iraq, was a hotly debated issue within the movement, much as it was in the country at large.

PALEO FACTION

Far more common than libertarian hawks were libertarians who reemphasized the generally antiwar orientation of the movement in the days after 9/11. Among them were many mainstream libertarians at organizations such as the Reason Foundation, as well as a distinct subset of the movement known as **PALEOLIBERTARIANS**. The paleolibertarians, largely centered on the Mises Institute, had in turn partnered since shortly after the Cold War with a subset of the conservative movement known as paleoconservatives. If both "neo" factions above tended to be globalist and hawkish in their outlook, both "paleo" fac-

tions tended to emphasize the value of local tradition and military isolationism.

For paleoconservatives, local tradition is sufficiently important that it can trump property rights on occasion, but the paleolibertarians would regard property rights as a constraint even on traditionalism. One arguable violation of property rights that both paleo camps tend to endorse, however, is controls on *immigration*.

The paleoconservatives might frankly argue against open borders on the grounds of cultural cohesion and traditionalism. But the paleolibertarians would argue only that, in a society already burdened with a welfare state, it is unfair to give taxpayers no say over which newcomers may end up drawing on resources from the system. The latter argument, it should be observed, pushes against the important libertarian assumption that people should be free to travel wherever they please, so long as they do not trespass on private property.

Non-paleo libertarians have accused paleolibertarians of merely finding a libertarian rationale for more primitive anti-immigrant sentiments. That accusation was made more plausible by the paleo faction's brief flirtation with racist and pro-militia rhetoric in the early 1990s, around the time of the federal government's heavy-handed, fatal Ruby Ridge and Waco raids against reclusive religious militants.

RON PAUL AND RAND PAUL

The emphases on borders, ethnicity, and the paleo alliance all subsided over the course of the next two decades, but not before being used as occasional rhetorical ammunition against the most prominent political figure to rise from the paleolibertarian faction: Texas congressman Ron Paul. After his failed 1988 Libertarian Party run for the presidency, Paul returned to the Republican Party and Congress, softened his stance on immigration, avoided conspiracy-theory rhetoric, and disavowed racist sentiments within the  paleo faction, including some controversial, apparently ghostwritten passages in his own newsletters from the early 90s.

Despite such baggage, Ron Paul began talking about his intention to run for the presidency again, this time as a Republican, immediately after the GOP once again lost control of Congress in 2006. Against the odds, this elderly, right-wing, pro-life, religious and tolerant, antiwar, anti-establishment Texan brought large numbers of young people into the libertarian movement—including an unprecedented number of women in what had historically been a disproportionately male movement. Although he did not win the Republican presidential nomination in either 2008 or 2012, he is widely acknowledged to have nudged the Republican Party in a slightly more libertarian, slightly less warlike direction.

Retiring from Congress after the second of his presidential runs, Ron Paul remained active as a writer and speaker on libertarian topics. He tirelessly promoted the Austrian School of economics, which had been his intellectual foundation in his early years of political activism during the 1970s within the "gold bug" movement. Adherents called for a return to the gold standard to curb inflation and the individual purchase of gold as a hedge against financial collapse.

Another important part of Ron Paul's legacy was his son Rand Paul, elected to the U.S. Senate as a Republican from Kentucky in 2010. That election year brought a national surge in "Tea Party" activism, which blended conservative and libertarian sentiments, often on the safe common ground of defense of the Constitution against encroaching big government. (The movement had a precedent in a 2007 Ron Paul speech at a Boston Tea Party anniversary event at Faneuil Hall.)

Rand Paul would himself run for the presidency in 2016, engaging in a precarious balancing act aimed at securing the support of a larger portion of Republican voters than the 10% his father had won over. Though Rand Paul's deviations from libertarian orthodoxy were few, he left some critics uncertain of how reliable and philosophically consistent he would be (not that that isn't a complaint about other politicians!).

Were his willingness to boost defense spending or to criticize a nuclear agreement with Iran signs that he would be significantly more hawkish than his father? Did his 2012 endorsement of Mitt Romney show that he was just another establishment Republican?

Despite such doubts, even ideological foes praised Rand Paul for drawing attention to issues rarely touched on by other Republicans, such as the militarization of police departments, the disparate racial impact of the Drug War, poverty in cities such as Detroit that might benefit from more free-market policies, mounting revelations about domestic spying by the National Security Agency and other arms of the surveillance state, and the controversial use of drone warfare.

Through it all, Rand Paul managed not just to bridge the libertarian/conservative ideological divide in a fashion that was more nearly paleoconservative than fusionist, he also gained a reputation for working across the aisle with Democrats in a friendly manner. His harshest critics may have been the neoconservatives and hawks in his own party.

Biography:
RON PAUL (1935–)

Born in Pittsburgh, Pennsylvania, to a German-American family, Paul became a physician in the 1960s, serving as a surgeon in the Air Force before entering private practice as a gynecologist in Texas. He credits President Nixon's decision to go off the gold standard in 1971 with inspiring him to go into politics. He was initially a participant in the "gold bug" movement of speakers and newsletter-writers who advocated private gold ownership and a return to the gold standard as means of discouraging the constant inflation of fiat, government-issued paper money, which central banks can print at will.

Paul shared these views with Murray Rothbard and other Austrian School-influenced economists and would go on to collaborate frequently with the Ludwig von Mises Institute, co-founded by Rothbard.

Paul carried his views to the U.S. Congress, where he served for decades as a representative from Texas (1976–1977, 1979–1985, and 1997–2013). He consistently voted against spending increases and militarism, routinely introducing attention-getting but doomed bills to abolish the Federal Reserve and achieve other libertarian ideals of limited — but growing — popularity.

Inspired by the gold bug movement, Paul also published newsletters about gold, investing, and politics that were sometimes inflected with the almost-apocalyptic or conspiratorial tone of the gold bug and survivalist movements. Often ghostwritten, some of the newsletters later earned him criticism for the perceived radicalism or racially insensitive tone of certain passages. Paul's own rhetoric in speeches changed over the decades, with early references to the malign influence of international advisory groups such as the Trilateral Commission giving way to broadly appealing libertarian messages and frequent invocation of the insights of the Austrian School of economics.

Frustrated by the big-government bent of even the Reagan-era Republican Party, Paul ran for president as the Libertarian Party candidate in 1988. After being returned to Congress, he later ran for president twice as a Republican, in 2008 and 2012. Though he did not receive the party's nomination in either year, he was widely credited with raising awareness of libertarian issues, increasing the number of participants in the libertarian movement, and nudging the GOP in a slightly more libertarian and slightly less militaristic direction.

After retiring from Congress in 2013, Paul continued to write and speak on libertarian topics through books, an online video service, nonprofit organizations, and a model school curriculum heavily influenced by libertarianism and partly influenced by millenarian Christian writers among Paul's colleagues.

LIBERALTARIANS

The attempt to coax a libertarian strain to life within the Republican Party came too late to satisfy some libertarians who wanted nothing more to do with conservatives and saw themselves as inheritors of the liberal, leftist, or anarchist traditions. Around 2007, shortly before the George W. Bush presidency ended, several began making their aversion to conservatism and the Republicans explicit, even as Ron Paul was preparing his Republican presidential run.

Cato Institute staffers Brink Lindsey and Will Wilkinson dubbed themselves "liberaltarians," as did participants in a group blog called Bleeding Heart Libertarians. Philosopher John Tomasi, like Wilkinson, promoted the idea of combining the free-market insights of Friedrich Hayek with the special attention to society's worst-off in the thinking of liberal philosopher John Rawls. (Wilkinson had called the combination "Rawlsekian".) Tomasi summed up a version of the view in his 2012 book *Free Market Fairness*.

Bleeding Heart Libertarians contributor Jacob Levy, a political scientist, not only placed himself within the liberal tradition but, in his 2015 book *Rationalism, Pluralism, & Freedom*, described a forgotten thread of liberalism that he positioned somewhere in between the strictly rationalist-individualist strain that produced both classical liberalism and libertarianism, and the rationalist-statist strain that produced twentieth-century welfare statism. This pluralist tradition, in a fashion akin to Alexis de Tocqueville, emphasized the importance of leaving small, intermediary groups, civil society institutions, and ethnic enclaves a large degree of freedom to order their own affairs rather than conforming to a single, state-decreed, nationwide norm.

Unfortunately, from Levy's perspective, a brief flowering in pluralist-liberal philosophy around the end of the nineteenth century was overlooked in the battle between declining classical (individualist) liberalism and rising modern (statist) liberalism of the sort advocated by socialism-influenced English philosophers L.T. Hobhouse and T.H. Green.

The "liberaltarians" are generally more accepting of minor welfare-statist violations of property rights than are conventional libertarians, especially for the purpose of aiding groups historically disadvantaged by the state or other forms of violence such as slavery.

THE IMPORTANCE OF CHOICE

While some libertarians leaned toward the right or left, *Reason* magazine and its website in the twenty-first century came to be edited by Matt Welch and Nick Gillespie, who eschewed strict philosophical analysis in favor of

approving broadly libertarian social trends. This was a more results-oriented, consequentialist take on libertarianism, which even led Gillespie to imply that people living in interesting, cosmopolitan areas are in some real sense more free than people living in boring rural areas, since they have more choices.

Valorizing choice and nonconformism, Gillespie and Welch co-authored the 2011 book *Declaration of Independents* about the ideological implications of American "independent" voters for the first time outnumbering either self-identified Republicans or self-identified Democrats. Here, they hoped, was the possible harbinger of a more fluid era of brief, single-issue coalitions and diminished political rigidity.

LEFT-LIBERTARIANISM

While the bulk of libertarians probably continued to think of themselves as libertarians in a very straightforward sense—requiring no prefixes, suffixes, or hyphens and hewing to the sort of mainstream libertarianism still favored at Cato and FEE—the social media boom of the 2010s fueled various more-obscure variations on libertar-

ian thought. Notable among these were various kinds of left-libertarians. The left-libertarians often share conventional leftists' view that inegalitarian social relationships, such as differing social roles for males and females (even if voluntary by conventional libertarian standards) are objectionable and marked by social injustice or unfair "privilege."

The ideological boundaries between such groups are ambiguous, but they arguably include *voluntaryists* and *mutualists.* They, like anarcho-capitalists, are entirely opposed to government, but some adhere to a model of economics similar to that held by the nineteenth-century anarchists mentioned earlier—in which capitalism is *also* viewed as either unnatural or unsustainable, with more communal (but strictly voluntary) modes of social organization morally preferable.

The think tank and media network Center for a Stateless Society describes itself as "free-market anarchist." Again in a fashion resembling nineteenth-century individualist anarchism, its contributors tend to object to the state in general as well as to condemn "capitalism" as it currently exists. They insist that companies would be smaller and more non-hierarchical in the absence of the state and even argue that "bossism," or the tendency for employers to behave in an authoritarian manner, would wither in the absence of the state. Many also share something like the old anarchist/Georgist aversion to landlords.

YOU KIDS WITH YOUR FACETWEETS AND VIDEO GAME TAPES! YOU HAVE NO RESPECT FOR MY INTELLECTUAL PROPERTY! STOP DOWNLOADING EVERYTHING! I'M AFRAID OF THE FUTURE AND REFUSE TO ADAPT TO THE MARKET!

PROPERTY RIGHTS AS BENCHMARK

It is not obvious that a diverse, free-market society can predictably deliver the specific cultural trends that any libertarian subgroup with a specific cultural agenda desires—whether it's Ayn Rand Objectivists who advocate atheism and egoism, or egalitarian feminists who want Objectivist Wall Streeters humbled. The important thing may be that all such factions continue to condemn the use of government (or other property rights violations) for achieving their ends.

Arguably, this makes all the culture-driven deviations from standard libertarianism beside the point. Once free to choose, people can form whatever cultural affinity groups they wish. So long as they continue to respect each other's property rights, it is *all* compatible with liberty. "Anything that's peaceful," as Leonard Read put it.

There will, of course, remain occasional disagreements over where exactly to draw the lines of property rights. Even mainstream libertarians who do not fall into any of the deviationist camps described above may disagree, for example, on whether fetuses are individuals with rights that must be protected; whether intellectual property as opposed to physical property is a legitimate construct (given that an idea can be copied without decreasing its availability to the original possessor); how to structure national defense (if at all); and what constitutes actionable environmental damage (and how to remedy it).

No matter what philosophical starting points or cultural endpoints different factions of libertarians emphasize, one can discern a common pattern among them: seeing property rights violations as an agreed-upon indicator of inappropriate behavior in nearly all situations. Property rights might not be the first thing to spring to a libertarian's mind in explaining his or her philosophical foundations, but they are the most reliable predictor of what actions and policies libertarians will accept or forbid. They enable most libertarians to predict what positions will be taken by the rest of the movement without even having to consult others—well befitting a movement of individualists.

Strong property rights might be bundled together with various other values by different factions, just as they often are by non-libertarian groups. But if strong property rights are desirable, it is reasonable to ask what would happen if they were literally never violated. There is at least one libertarian faction willing to take the philosophy to that radical yet logical conclusion, advocating the complete abolition of government: the aforementioned anarcho-capitalists. We turn to them last.

ANARCHO-
CAPITALISM
7

TAKING IT ALL THE WAY

JUST AS MANY MOVEMENTS EXPE-
rience a tension between outreach and purity, so
too has libertarianism experienced frequent internal
debate over whether to recruit people
by softening its rhetoric—or even by
altering and softening its principles (as
perhaps "liberaltarians" do). Libertarians arguably spent a generation after the
Cold War seeking ways to soften their
message in order to gain mainstream accep-

tance. And yet, by the second decade of the twenty-first
century, the most hardcore and uncompromising version
of libertarianism seemed to be one of the fastest-growing,
namely anarcho-capitalism.

Perhaps there is more outreach value in sticking to one's

guns than there appears at first, especially in an age with less and less patience for nuance. After all, it is often when libertarians attempt to compromise that they are attacked most. They are accused of being tools of the Republicans if they forgive state expenditures done in the name of running courts, cops, and the military. And they are charged with accepting a more expansive state if they accept the logic underlying such policies as affirmative action or unemployment insurance.

In addition to Rothbard's anarcho-capitalist phase (arguably abandoned when he became part of the Mises Institute's paleolibertarian push), libertarianism has been influenced by the thinking of Milton Friedman's son, **DAVID FRIEDMAN,** and his anarcho-capitalist 1973 book *Machinery of Freedom*. Slightly more Chicago School than Rothbard's approach, the younger Friedman's book weighs the pros and cons of privatizing state functions in case after case, showing in a nearly utilitarian way how adherence to strict property rights could resolve dilemma after dilemma, including the private provision of defense.

THE MILITARY

There are already mercenaries who perform the same basic function as government-run armies. And there is no reason in principle that a vast number of subscribers could not hire a large mercenary army, even on an ongoing basis, to protect their homes and their surroundings from potential invaders. Of course, given the great success of guerrilla armies over the centuries, everywhere from Colonial America to Afghanistan, it's not clear that a big, centralized command-and-control army is the most effective deterrent to invasion. Would we be safer with a decentralized, less predictable means of fighting back? If you were an invading Chinese army, would you rather get Washington, D.C. to surrender and call it a day or risk spending years fighting house to house across a continent, never knowing for sure if or when the enemy would stop?

A further benefit of an all-subscriber military is that there would be far less incentive for it to engage in provocative behavior. Some conflicts aren't worth getting into, but a big government with the power to tax and conscript people is less likely to remember that. It may be more prone to

VAMPIRE FOR HIRE.

exaggerate the need to defend the national honor against minor slights, leading to destructive, large-scale wars. The sweeping anarchist opposition to standing armies in the early twentieth century struck most critics as reckless, but would the results of doing things the anarchists' way have been any worse than the pointless Great War that purportedly defensive militaries in Europe dragged the world into from 1914 to 1918?

POLICE

If military defense is possible without government, surely everyday policing is even easier. We already have security guards for hire, after all. And there is no reason to believe that competing security companies must resolve every disagreement by shooting at each other on the spot. We already live in a world in which there are overlapping police jurisdictions, and (even in a government-run world) many cases are resolved by some nonviolent method of dispute resolution, since each police department recognizes the potentially high cost of failure to cooperate.

In the view of anarcho-capitalists, even market-loving Ayn Rand and libertarian philospher **ROBERT NOZICK** may have been hasty in thinking that competing police services would tend to fight each other whenever they disagree. (As a result, Rand, Nozick, and other minarchists may have unnecessarily retained elements of

statist thinking.) Nozick's 1974 book *Anarchy, State, and Utopia* is nearly Rothbardian in its assumption that people should be treated as if they have unassailable property rights. But he also argues that competing police services inevitably would fight or threaten each other until one came to dominate and proclaim itself a monopoly provider of security. At that point it is at least a minimal state.

Nozick may have underestimated the desire of diverse customers to keep paying for diverse protection agencies (such as, perhaps, cops specializing in preventing attacks on ethnic minorities in areas where that's a common problem). And he may also underestimate the ability of protection agencies to see that they might live and profit longer by tolerating each other rather than by entering other companies' headquarters with guns blazing. Richer though some protection agencies may be than others, defense, like guerrilla warfare, is relatively cheap. Even if a billionaire hires ninjas to kill you, he increases his odds of being shot later by one of your vengeful relatives. Is it really worth it to him?

Think, too, of the many problems associated with existing government-run police that could be alleviated by privatizing them. For one thing, competing police services could not adopt the lazy attitude that there is no one to arrest them if they misbehave. Another police company might well do so. Under current conditions, the domination of a given geographic area by a single police department opens the door to inertia, corruption, and racism.

ADJUDICATION

Most sane people would prefer to settle large-scale disagreements in court rather than on the field of combat—and they can do so even in the absence of government. Already there are arbitration firms, often used by financial institutions and other businesses that seek quicker dispute resolution than that provided by government courts. These firms must render consistently just decisions if they want to maintain their reputations as good arbitrators. In the event one party to a dispute refuses to submit to any court, the venue could be left up to the discretion of the other party.

A mere century or two ago, notes David Friedman, justice in places as familiar as England was often handled in this way. It wasn't until the early nineteenth century that standing police departments run by government became the norm. And when they did, critics often charged that the administration of justice had gotten *worse* than it had been in the days of private courts.

The possibility of private arbitration firms also means that very sophisticated cases could be tried without a government court system. Even environmental pollution claims (property violations if there is detectable damage to buildings or lungs or the trees someone owns) in theory could be handled via *class-action suits* on behalf of all the poisoned parties against a selection of major polluters. Many people say they hate lawyers, but lawsuits have the advantage of requiring people to demonstrate that some sort of harm was done, whereas regulations merely have to sound good in the political speeches that inspired their passage.

On Practicality and Limits

The anarcho-capitalist vision is admittedly radical, but it may also be easier and more practical than trying to run

Biography:
ROBERT NOZICK (1938-2002)

Within economics, libertarianism remains

a minority view. Outside economics, it is even rarer for libertarian voices to prevail. One relatively rare case of a libertarian rising to prominence in academic philosophy in recent decades is that of Robert Nozick. Born in New York City and educated at Columbia, Princeton, and Oxford, he went on to teach philosophy at Harvard, teaching one of his final courses jointly with law professor Alan Dershowitz and paleontologist Stephen Jay Gould.

Nozick described himself in his best-known work, *Anarchy, State, and Utopia* (1974), as being drawn reluctantly to libertarian conclusions despite not fully liking the company in which he thereby found himself. He makes the case in that book that strong property rights lead logically to the moral impermissibility of anything more than a minimal state. Initially there will be competing subscriber protection agencies in a world where taxes are morally rejected, but in time, he thought, one protection agency may come to dominate and thus become a de facto minimal government with a monopoly on force.

Along the way, and with an abiding openness to counter-arguments, Nozick defended such other core libertarian notions as the moral permissibility of profit.

He noted that if Wilt Chamberlain accepted even a tiny amount of money from each of thousands of fans to watch him shoot basketballs, Chamberlain would emerge rich — and each of his fans would have slightly fewer dollars than they did before the transactions but would consider themselves better off.

Because Nozick was willing to admit the flexibility and uncertainty of philosophical arguments in general, he was sufficiently admired by thinkers of other schools of thought to be taught in dialogue with them. *Anarchy, State, and Utopia* is often used in academic philosophy classes as a counterpoint to left-liberal philosopher John Rawls' *A Theory of Justice* (1971), which used comparably detailed deductions to derive a system resembling the contemporary welfare state.

Among Nozick's nonpolitical thought experiments that continue to echo in philosophy are the dilemma of the "utility monster," a hypothetical person whose joys and pains are far greater than those of his fellow citizens and who may therefore deserve special moral consideration; and the dilemma of the "experience machine" (similar to a question posed in the film *The Matrix*), in which one must decide whether the illusion of a perfect life is truly preferable to confronting reality as it is, even if it contains pain and hardship.

The Examined Life (1989), a collection of philosophical essays, includes "The Zig-zag of Politics," in which Nozick still praises libertarian views but concedes that justice or freedom might be part of a larger package of plural values, some of which cannot be reconciled with perfect coherence and certainty.

the world by means of government. And it might make the world more peaceful and prosperous. The anarcho-capitalist system is also a far cry from mere "fiscal conservatism," if that implies tolerance of the web of subsidies, protec-

tionist tariffs, crony-crafted regulations, Federal Reserve currency-manipulation, and bailouts that characterize the current economy. Anarcho-capitalists call for a radical change in our method of governance—indeed the end of governance, in a sense—while many fiscal conservatives talk big but balk at almost any policy change that might cause a temporary downturn in the stock market. To the anarcho-capitalist, that's no way to bring about real change.

Of course, traditional or "left" anarchists insist that anarcho-capitalism is nonsense, that a true anarchist rejects both government and capitalism. Certainly the participation of self-proclaimed anarchists over the course of the twentieth and early twenty-first centuries in pro-Soviet, anti-global-trade, and Occupy movements suggests that most conventional anarchists are not capitalists. Anarcho-capitalists, however, might respond that conventional anarchists should simply imagine a world entirely devoid of government, such as both factions want, and ask themselves what rules of conduct they would recommend to the inhabitants of the new anarchist world.

Does an individual in that world have the right to respond to personal assault with sufficient force to defend himself? Does he have a right to manipulate some portion of the material world without having to plead with the mob each time before undertaking an action? If so, it appears that our hypothetical inhabitant of the anarchist future has de facto property rights. It appears that, as posited at the outset of this book, he has the right to defend himself from assault, theft, and fraud. And if we agree on that and allow him to collaborate with other willing individuals to use and defend his rights, we have all become anarcho-capitalists.

Of course, under anarcho-capitalism or indeed any milder form of libertarian regime, there will always be

the final anarchic option if some unlikely nightmare scenario comes to pass. It will always be possible to *break* the
rules this book has described in such detail. Humanity
never truly loses that fundamental ability. Indeed it may be
easier to overturn the laws of a libertarian society than to
prevent the myriad tragedies that already occur on a daily
basis thanks to thick bureaucracy in democratic regimes.
Even the "post-anarchists"—who add deconstructionist
and poststructuralist uncertainty about truth itself to their
antipathy for government and capitalism—may not fully
appreciate the residual freedom we always have to say that
the system isn't working and must be discarded.

As a first step, though, before we find ourselves in a
world with no government at all, libertarians of all stripes
ask you to contemplate a world with *less* government. It
may turn out that the system of control and redistribution
that we thought was working to solve our problems was
the real problem all along.

TEN DILEMMAS
8 FOR LIBERTARIANS

BEING CONFIDENT THAT PROP-
erty rights are the proper framework for a law code
does not mean that libertarians think that no ambiguous
or tricky situations can arise under such a law code. Some
areas of frequent debate—not necessarily insoluble ones—
even among ardent defenders of strong property rights
include the following (in no particular order):

Status of Intellectual Property

If the underlying rationale for the establishment of property rights is that physical resources
are scarce (which for economists merely means less than
infinitely abundant), but an idea can be copied without
destroying the original idea, perhaps it is unnecessary to
turn ideas into property.

On the other hand, if there are important benefits from
having to generate one's own ideas, such as spurring greater

originality and innovation, perhaps there is rule-utilitarian justification for establishing property in this area, as well as a metaphysical rebuke to what Ayn Rand would call parasites and second-handers.

(Note: If copyrights and/or patents were abolished, elaborate trade-secret agreements might still be worked out on an individual contractual basis.)

Monopolies

Austrian School economists note that true monopolies are rare or non-existent in markets, usually arising only as a result of government-granted licenses and privileges, not market transactions alone. If companies become lazier and less efficient with increasing size, they will tend to raise prices—the great fear of critics of monopolies—but in so doing will encourage upstart rival companies to swoop in and take away their customers by charging less or offering innovative alternative services.

However, Chicago School economists sometimes note that antitrust laws could in principle foster competition and efficiency in the unlikely event that the laws were effectively administered. And they note (somewhat like the Georgists with their skepticism about land ownership) that there can be monopolies in extremely scarce resources, if, for instance, the world has very few accessible diamond mines.

PRIVATE PRISONS

Partial privatization can sometimes produce worse results than government control, and while great efficiencies can be achieved from government "contracting out" services to private providers, perverse incentives can also be created if those private providers are still permitted to lobby the government for greater (taxpayer-funded) use of their services. In the case of private prisons, it can even mean lobbying by the private providers for laws (such as long prison sentences for drug use) that impinge on people's freedom in ways far more intrusive than the budgetary bloat that privatization was meant to address.

CULTURAL ATTITUDES

There is broad agreement among libertarians of different schools that government should be reduced and that individuals' bodies and property should rarely or never be interfered with by the law or other individuals. Beyond that, strictly speaking, a libertarian might hold any number of cultural attitudes, from Christian to atheist, from traditionalist to avant-gardist, from sexist to feminist, from lover of American culture to island-dwelling Malay-influenced Buddhist.

Naturally, however, there is a tendency for different libertarians to argue that their own cultural allegiances are the ones most apt to facilitate a love of liberty throughout society. There is no clear consensus as to whether, say, Victorian prudery or hippie free-spiritedness is more compatible with a sustained commitment to libertarianism; a historical case could be made for either.

EMERGENCY SITUATIONS

Most people of all ideological stripes, including libertarians, acknowledge that there could, at least hypothetically, be emergencies so dire that they warrant temporary violations of the usual ethical or legal rules. Few libertarians would oppose stealing a ray gun that was the only means of disintegrating a meteor on the verge of destroying the

Earth if the suicidal owner refused to use it and there were no other means of salvation.

The critical question, of course, is how many such emergency situations to acknowledge. Acknowledge too many and the rules cease to be rules. In nearly all situations, libertarians will tend to treat property rights as inviolable, recognizing the long-term benefits of maintaining such a system.

CRONYISM/PROTECTIONISM

No libertarian would hesitate to condemn government subsidies and bailouts for corporations or, for that matter, special regulatory (or tariff) punishments inflicted on the corporations' rivals. Given the pervasive nature of such legal arrangements, though, it is difficult to know with certainty what a market devoid of deformations by government would look like.

How much of current corporate behavior is admirable, meritocratic, and likely to endure in the absence of government as we know it? How resistant to a true free market would most companies be if they faced the potential political transformation of the current regime?

NOISE POLLUTION

While punches and gunshots are relatively easy to detect and police, mere communication—of unwelcome ideas or even non-threatening epithets—is not something libertarians want policed at all. But what about loud noises, especially in residential areas? Noise is vibration, after all, and at some level can even cause physical pain. How much is too much? Libertarians might well defer to common law, evolved on a case-by-case basis, to settle such questions, but there is no obvious perfect solution.

CONVENTIONAL POLLUTION

Mises Institute chairman Lew Rockwell has insisted that the permissible level of pollution in a libertarian society is "zero," since no one, including a factory-owning industrialist, has the right to render filthy someone else's property. Rather than the end of all industrial production, this might simply mean that more effort should be put into capturing effluents and exhaust (to the delight of conventional environmentalists, not just *free-market environmentalists*).

For a circumstance to be legally actionable, however, some harm ought to be demonstrated, and most libertarians are wary of regulations or activist campaigns that simply assume minuscule chemical or other residues to be harmful. If the damage done is zero, invisible fumes may not warrant legal intervention.

MENTAL COMPETENCE AND THE STATUS OF CHILDREN

Like most modern political philosophies, libertarianism is a model largely built around the assumption that the moral agents described are competent adults, capable at least on occasion of making reasoned decisions. It is unclear in most philosophies at what age people become competent decision-makers who ought to be both free and accountable for the consequences of their actions. Some

libertarians are content to defer to the standard legal age of adulthood, while others think even children should be able to assert their freedom from either governmental or parental control.

Similarly, it is unclear at what point a libertarian should consider someone so impaired by mental illness (possibly including senility) as to cease being a competent decision-maker and perhaps deserve different legal rights (greater in some respects, diminished in others).

The influential libertarian psychiatrist Thomas Szasz (1920–2012) argued that "mental illness" has no clear meaning and that no matter how strange some people's decisions or decision-making processes, they should remain free so long as they do not harm others. Szasz and his point of view had a major influence on the U.S. de-institutionalization movement of the late twentieth century, after decades of holding even harmless mentally ill people against their will.

IMMIGRATION

Most libertarians believe that people should be able to migrate freely without regard to (government-decreed) national borders, so long as they do not enter private property without permission. Some, however, especially paleolibertarians, see the potential drain on collectivized resources as a reason to let current taxpayers decide who may enter the system and thus who will be allowed to cross the border. Many acknowledge that in an ideal, free-market system, people would be able to move about at will but argue that we must abolish the welfare state prior to adopting open borders.

The case against open borders may actually be stronger for tiny polities, such as Hong Kong or the recently declared Balkan micronation of Liberland, which could more easily be swamped or legally altered by an influx of socialistic voters than could a large nation such as the United States.

MAJOR LIBERTARIAN
9 SCHOOLS of THOUGHT

THERE IS A GREAT DEAL OF overlap among libertarian factions and much ambiguity about dividing lines between libertarian factions, as well as between these factions and associated non-libertarian groups. With apologies to everyone left out or glossed over, here are some of the most prominent groups identified with the broader libertarian movement:

agorists: Founded by writer/activist Samuel E. Konkin III (a.k.a. SEK3, 1947–2004), agorism resembles anarcho-capitalism but stripped of compromises with mainstream commercial society. Agorists reject as immoral, for instance, not just the levying of taxes by government but the paying of taxes by citizens and the collecting of sales tax by businesses. Agorists valorize underground, black market activities or "counter-economics."

anarcho-capitalists: Anarcho-capitalism calls for strict adhererence to the rule against violating property rights. Even what most libertarians consider "legitimate" functions of government are abolished in favor of private mechanisms, leaving no government at all (that is, "anarchism" plus "capitalism").

Austrian School economists: The "Austrians," following in the footsteps of Carl Menger, Ludwig von Mises, and Friedrich Hayek, emphasize the subjectivity of economic valuations and thus methodological individualism, leading them to have little patience for the use of vast statistical aggregates and macroeconomic generalizations in setting policy.

Chicago School economists: More conventional than the "Austrians," adherents of the Chicago School, such as Milton Friedman, tend to embrace at least some conventional macroeconomic and neoclassical assumptions about how to do economics, paying attention to factors such as aggregate demand and the stimulus effects of increasing the currency supply while still urging free-market-oriented policies.

classical liberals: The eighteenth- and nineteenth-century forebears of the libertarian movement, the classical liberals were less doctrinaire than today's libertarians but emphasized individualism, free markets, and constitutionalism rather than the welfare-state approaches popularized by twentieth-century liberals.

Dark Enlightenment: More an assortment of non-libertarians and former libertarians, many participants in this small movement accept the basic libertarian description of economics but believe that society since the eighteenth-century Enlightenment has rendered taboo some of the most important truths about social reality, ones that render conventional libertarian-ism an unworkable ideal. They argue that the enduring appeal of monarchy and religion, the ineffectual nature of democracy, and the existence of important ethnic and gender differences all make simple individualism naïve.

geolibertarians: Some libertarians incorporate into their thinking the skepticism expressed by nineteenth-century econo-mist and politician Henry George about the moral acceptability of land ownership. Geolibertarians may also emphasize stew-ardship of land in an environmentalist sense.

left-libertarians: An array of libertarians, often anarcho-capitalist and associated with organizations such as the Alliance of the Libertarian Left, the Molinari Society, and the Center for a Stateless Society, left-libertarians urge the abolition not only of the state but (by voluntary means) of various inegalitarian relationships in the marketplace, such as that between landlords and tenants, bosses and workers, or traditional patriarchal hus-bands and wives. The left-libertarians include many feminists and so-called voluntaryists and mutualists.

liberaltarians: Often associated with academia or think tanks, the liberaltarians urge tempering the strict property rights adherence—and sometimes harsh rhetoric—of the lib-ertarian movement along modern-liberal lines, possibly via acceptance of government policies such as affirmative action, unemployment benefits, or a guaranteed minimum income. They often seek to justify libertarian positions in terms pal-atable to welfare-state liberals in the tradition of John Rawls, gauging market policies in part by their effect on the poor and traditionally marginalized populations.

Libertarian Party: Since the 1970s, the Libertarian Party has placed a few candidates in low-level offices but has had little success at the national level. Most libertarians are not Libertarian Party members, but many regard it as a useful awareness-raising tool. Others regard it as foolhardy or, given that some libertarians morally oppose voting, even un-libertarian.

libertarians: It warrants noting that many, perhaps most, libertarians still regard themselves as libertarians in a straightforward, factionless sense: supportive of any reduction in the size and power of government without entering into divisive battles over which methods are best or what comes next.

minarchists: Most libertarians are not anarchists, advocating a minimal, limited, "night watchman" state rather than no state at all. The limited state is usually assumed to have little more than courts, police, and a purely defensive military among its legitimate functions. Those functions, it is usually expected, should be clearly spelled out in a constitution to prevent runaway government expansion. The United States began as a more or less minarchist system.

neolibertarians: This term has been used in two unrelated senses, both obscure: to indicate libertarians who are not geo-libertarians and to indicate libertarians who, somewhat like neoconservatives, believe in a significant role for the military in policing conflicts and combating tyranny in other nations.

Objectivists: Followers of the philosophy of Ayn Rand, the large Objectivist movement rejects big government but also, in most formulations, anarchism as well as religion and other elements of culture and conventional morality, including altruism (properly understood). Many Objectivists reject the label "libertarian," though Objectivists are best understood as people who are libertarians but are other things in addition and see their political, moral, and metaphysical views as interwoven.

paleolibertarians: Importing ideas from the Old Right and contemporary paleoconservatives (who admire local traditions and eschew globalism), paleolibertarians often adopt a populist, declinist cultural narrative about the United States, lamenting its transformation from republic to warlike empire, its growing crony-capitalist tendencies, and its unfortunate transformation by mass immigration. Unlike many libertarians, they tend to see immigration-limiting border enforcement as a legitimate function of government. The Mises Institute in Alabama and Ron Paul have espoused paleolibertarian views.

SIDENOTE: The **TEA PARTY** movement is not predominantly libertarian but has a significant libertarian streak. Often seen as beginning in 2009 with Wall Streeters' rejection of Obama policies—and having a 2007 Boston Tea Party commemorative gathering as a precursor—the movement urged the Republican Party to stick to its principles, some socially conservative and some fiscally conservative or libertarian, but generally anti-big-government. Rand Paul described his election to the U.S. Senate in 2010 as a victory for the Tea Party and said that the federal debt was the movement's top priority.

Q *Do libertarians think markets can do no wrong?*

A Humans make mistakes. They can make purchases they later regret. They can cheer on social trends about which they later grow skeptical. They can even make money by selling books about how to destroy market economies. But the important question for purposes of judging libertarianism relative to other philosophies is whether there is any reason to expect that government intervention would consistently produce better outcomes. Libertarians think that is doubtful, especially given the likelihood that government, having extended its power in some way, will go on to apply it to other problems for which it is even less suited. Markets aren't perfect. And government, according to libertarians, is worse.

LIBERTARIANISM for Beginners

Q *Do libertarians really think they're going to take over the government?*

A Although the 1% of votes for Libertarian Party candidates in U.S. presidential elections is not necessarily the best indicator of broader libertarian sentiment (and even broader libertarian-compatible sentiment) in society, it's a reminder that big government views are still very, very popular. Libertarians see the great likelihood of insolvency and loss of credibility for overspending big governments, but they know that doesn't necessarily produce a coherent philosophical revolution. Still, pushing for more freedom whenever possible beats pushing in the wrong direction, toward tyranny.

Q *Do libertarians want everyone to have guns?*

A Since libertarians recognize each person's right to self-defense and each person's right to own whatever property she chooses—and do not think that person has committed a crime unless doing harm to someone else—libertarians recognize the *right* to own guns but of course do not insist people take any particular attitude toward guns. For instance, one might ardently defend the right to own guns without enjoying all manifestations of "gun culture."

Libertarians would prefer to see conflicts settled without guns but are mindful of the fact that if no ordinary law-abiding citizens own guns, all weapons will be in the hands of criminals and the state—a dangerous situation.

Q *Do libertarians think that making money is all that matters—not art or family or love?*

A Libertarians think every aspect of human life matters. In order to allow people to work out how to handle all those other matters in the ways they find most rewarding, they believe, it is best to keep government out of it all. Comedy matters, for example, but we do not prove our concern for comedy by handing over the control of jokes to a Department of Jokes. Libertarians hold that diverse free individuals can better innovate and cooperate than any government committee. Let the law stick to preventing people from injuring and robbing each other, already a big job. Meanwhile, some people will use their freedom to make money, some to be monks, some to study, and some to change their lifestyle from year to year. Let them all do as they please.

Q *Shouldn't we put [nationalism, duty, military honor, manifest destiny, solidarity, equality, you name it] before individual happiness?*

A Perhaps, but the burden is on the person who supports those other things to explain why they are worth sacrificing human happiness (not just short-term happiness but long-term, overall happiness for the human race as a whole). Asserting that any of those things matter so much that humans must be sacrificed to it seems like a betrayal of the human race to something alien.

Q *Do libertarians have a special fondness for science fiction?*

A Widely regarded as a movement that attracted "nerds" in the late twentieth and early twenty-first centuries, including many computer programmers, libertarianism's ranks have included a rich complement of sci-fi fans and more than a few sci-fi authors. Among the latter are Neal Stephenson, L. Neil Smith, Poul Anderson, Jerry Pournelle, Vernor Vinge, and, perhaps most important, Robert Heinlein (whose 1966 book *The Moon Is a Harsh Mistress* depicts an anarcho-capitalist revolution on the Moon and mentions Objectivists sympathetically). The anarchist sci-fi writer Robert Anton Wilson touched on a number of themes of interest to libertarians as well.

CHRONOLOGY

SOMETIMES CALLED REVI-
sionists or conspiracy theorists, libertari-
ans are usually just looking at different causal aspects of
history than pro-government history writers. The deeds
of kings, presidents, and military leaders may not look as
heroic through a libertarian lens.

Although human freedom and technology both have
made great strides in some ways, in other ways recent centuries have seen a reduction in human freedom. Certainly
the twentieth century saw the spread of several big-government ideologies opposed to libertarian ideals, individualism, and free markets.

In just a few decades around the start of the twentieth
century, *Progressives* blended big business and big government thinking in the United States; financiers and
politicians collaborated to give the U.S. an influential
central bank in the form of the *Federal Reserve*; Russia
and then China were overtaken by *Communism*; Western
Europe was overrun by *fascism*; Western nations devel-

oped massive *military-industrial complexes*; and *conservatism* gradually became more accepting and supportive of these trends, slowly shedding its early-twentieth-century libertarian and anti-militarist tendencies. Even *anarchism*, by definition anti-government, became pro-Soviet in the early twentieth century; by the late twentieth century it often focused on interfering with global trade.

Despite statism's grievous missteps, libertarianism has not swept the globe over the past century. Still, alongside the history of increasing acceptance of big government has been a series of events, often less noticed, making up a chronology of libertarianism:

1647–1650	Levellers movement active in England
1688	Glorious Revolution replaces English monarch
1689	John Locke's *Two Treatises of Government*
1756	Edmund Burke's (proto-anarchist) *A Vindication of Natural Society*
1759	Adam Smith's *Theory of Moral Sentiments*
1776	Adam Smith's *Wealth of Nations*
1776	signing of the American Declaration of Independence
1787–1789	writing and ratification of the U.S. Constitution
1787–1788	publication of *The Federalist Papers* defending the U.S. Constitution
1790	Edmund Burke's (conservative) *Reflections on the Revolution in France*
1859	John Stuart Mill's *On Liberty*
1865	U.S. slavery effectively ended by Confederacy's surrender
1867	U.S. anarchist Lysander Spooner publishes his *No Treason* pamphlets (Nos. 1, 2, and 6), including "The Constitution of No Authority"

1881–1908   U.S. individualist anarchist magazine *Liberty* published by Benjamin Tucker

1883   communist philosopher Karl Marx dies

1883   Carl Menger publishes *Investigations into the Method of the Social Sciences with Special Reference to Economics*, explaining the disagreement of what would come to be called the Austrian School of economics with the methodology of the German historicists

1895   Eugen Böhm von Bawerk becomes Austrian minister of finance, fighting to maintain the gold standard and cut the government budget

1912   Ludwig von Mises' *Theory of Money and Credit*

1914   World War I begins

1926   H.L. Mencken's *Notes on Democracy*

1935   Albert Jay Nock's *Our Enemy, the State*

1940   Mises emigrates to the United States

1943   Rose Wilder Lane's *The Discovery of Freedom*

1943   Isabel Paterson's *The God of the Machine*

1943   Ayn Rand's *The Fountainhead*

1944   Friedrich Hayek's *Road to Serfdom*

1946   Foundation for Economic Education (FEE) founded

1946   Henry Hazlitt's Bastiat-influenced *Economics in One Lesson*

1946   Milton Friedman accepts an offer to teach at the University of Chicago

1947   in Switzerland, first meeting of the Mont Pelerin Society

1949   Mises' *Human Action*

1953   Intercollegiate Society of Individualists founded by combination of libertarians and conservatives, including William F. Buckley. (It later becomes the more conservative Intercollegiate Studies Institute.)

1957   Ayn Rand's *Atlas Shrugged*

1961   libertarian academic networking organization Institute for Humane Studies founded by F.A. "Baldy" Harper

1964	Friedman an advisor to the Barry Goldwater presidential campaign
1968	*Reason* magazine founded by Lanny Friedlander
1971	Libertarian Party founded
1972	Laissez-Faire Books founded
1973	David D. Friedman's *Machinery of Freedom*
1973	Murray Rothbard's *For a New Liberty*
1974	Robert Nozick's *Anarchy, State, and Utopia*
1974	Cato Institute founded by Ed Crane, Charles Koch, and Murray Rothbard
1974	Friedrich Hayek receives Nobel Prize in Economics
1976	Milton Friedman receives Nobel Prize in Economics
1980	Thomas Sowell's *Knowledge and Decisions*
1982	Ludwig von Mises Institute founded
1984	Competitive Enterprise Institute founded
1986	James Buchanan receives Nobel Prize in Economics
1986	Independent Institute founded
1987	*Liberty* magazine founded
1989	European Communism collapses; Berlin Wall breached
1989	John Stossel's first overtly libertarian TV news segment, "Relaxing the Rules"
1992	Gary Becker receives Nobel Prize in Economics
1998	Virginia Postrel's *The Future and Its Enemies*
2002	Vernon Smith receives Nobel Prize in Economics
2008, 2012	Rep. Ron Paul's campaigns for the Republican Party presidential nomination (Students for Liberty and Young Americans for Liberty founded)
2010–2011	Judge Andrew Napolitano hosts *FreedomWatch* on Fox Business Network
2010	Tea Party influences U.S. congressional elections
2016	Sen. Rand Paul's campaign for the Republican Party presidential nomination

GLOSSARY

agorist: believing in the practice of counter-economics or frequent recourse to black-market activity instead of government or even government-regulated firms

anarchist: opposed to the existence of government

anarcho-capitalist: opposed to the existence of government and in favor of property rights adherence and thus the existence of markets

arbitration firm: a private dispute-settling service comparable to a court

assault, theft, and fraud: the three main categories of crime in Roman-influenced law codes and the only three things forbidden by a strictly libertarian law code

cartel: an attempt among businesses without a common owner to collaborate to keep prices high or by agreement to avoid introducing competing new services; non-governmental cartels tend to erode quickly as the participants find new, subtle ways to compete with each other and the cartel unravels

catallaxy: the economy understood, as in the Austrian School conception, as a confluence of divergent individual preferences and unplanned emergent orders rather than a discernible universal plan or tendency

coercion: any violation of a person's property rights or bodily integrity by means of an explicit or implicit threat of force; the initiation of force against a non-aggressor

cost-benefit analysis: the often-neglected utilitarian or economic weighing of a policy or an action's positive consequences against its negative consequences

democracy: majority rule, as for example two wolves and a sheep voting on what to have for dinner

diffuse costs: the deceptively widespread costs imposed on all or most members of society, as by taxation, to pay for concentrated benefits, such as a subsidy to one firm or a monument seen by the inhabitants of one neighborhood, who will tend to lobby harder than the people bearing the less-perceptible cost of the project

laissez-faire: from the French for "allow to do," the attitude of minimal government interference in business and markets

minarchist: believing in a small, limited government with well-defined, usually constitutionally constrained duties (*min*imal as opposed to *an*archic)

natural rights: forms of moral respect, including respect for each other's autonomy, that all moral agents owe each other. The natural rights adherent, as opposed to the rule utilitarian, would deny that rights are dependent upon their practical consequences.

natural law: a universal moral framework and social order that is well-functioning, sustainable, and presumably codified, as in the U.S. Constitution. As a framework broader than natural rights alone, natural law appears in the thinking of philosophers influenced by Aristotle or Catholicism. As invoked by libertarians, natural law does not trump natural rights but provides a context for them.

non-aggression principle (NAP): shorthand common among radical libertarians—especially anarcho-capitalists and/or Libertarian Party activists—for the view that one should never violate another person's property rights or bodily integrity. Rather than seeing taxes, for instance, as a matter for complex policy analysis, strict NAP adherents would tend to say "taxation is theft."

protection agency: the anarcho-capitalist alternative to a government-run police department; private police

regulatory capture: the tendency, as during the New Deal, for dominant industries to collaborate with and steer to their own advantage (and to the disadvantage of rivals) the government agencies intended to rein them in

rent-seeking: attempting to gain profits merely from possessing some advantage or connection rather than by producing new value

spontaneous order: social organization, as of markets or institutions, without planning by a central, controlling force

supernormal profits: profits greatly in excess of the 6% or so that corporations typically average, usually indicative either of a short-term advantage conferred by some novel business practice or a special advantage conferred by government; unlikely to last long in a free market, where firms keep competing to offer (among other things) lower prices and thereby secure a larger portion of available customers than rivals, making profits tend over time toward zero, all else being equal and absent innovations and new services

utilitarianism: popularized by Jeremy Bentham, James Mill, and classical liberal philosopher John Stuart Mill, the view that morality consists of maximizing the long-term happiness of all morally relevant agents (all humans, perhaps other animals). "Rule utilitarians," as opposed to "act utilitarians," believe that it is dangerous to encourage people to gauge the utility of each individual action anew and so encourage sticking to moral and legal rules—such as property rights—that tend to foster increased happiness.

FURTHER READING

Bastiat, Frederic. *The Law*. Eastford, CT: Martino Fine Books, 2011.

Doherty, Brian. *Radicals for Capitalism: A Freewheeling History of the Modern American Libertarian Movement*. New York: PublicAffairs, 2007.

Friedman, Milton and Rose. *Free to Choose: A Personal Statement*. New York: Harcourt, 1980.

Hazlitt, Henry. *Economics in One Lesson: The Shortest and Surest Way to Understand Basic Economics*. New York: Crown Business, 1988.

Hayek, Friedrich. *The Road to Serfdom*. Chicago: University of Chicago Press, 2007.

Hayek, Friedrich. *The Constitution of Liberty: The Definitive Edition*. Chicago: University of Chicago Press, 2011.

Konkin III, Samuel E. *New Libertarian Manifesto*. Huntington Beach, CA: Koman Publishing, 1983.

Mill, John Stuart. *On Liberty*. Mineola, NY: Dover Thrift Editions, 2002.

Mises, Ludwig von. *Human Action*. Auburn, AL: Mises Institute, 2010.

Mises, Ludwig von. *Socialism*. Indianapolis: Liberty Classics, 1981.

Murray, Charles. *What It Means to Be a Libertarian: A Personal Interpretation*. New York: Broadway Books, 1996.

Narveson, Jan. *The Libertarian Idea*. Philadelphia: Temple University Press, 1988.

Nozick, Robert. *Anarchy, State, and Utopia*. New York: Basic Books, 2011.

Rand, Ayn, with Alan Greenspan, Nathaniel Branden, and Robert Hessen. *Capitalism: The Unknown Ideal*. New York: Signet, 1986.

Rothbard, Murray N. *For a New Liberty: The Libertarian Manifesto*. Auburn, AL: Mises Institute, 2011.

Spencer, Herbert. *Social Statics, or The Conditions essential to Happiness specified, and the First of them Developed*. New York: Robert Schalkenbach Foundation, 1995.

Tuccille, Jerome. *It Usually Begins with Ayn Rand: An Oral History of the Libertarian Movement*. New York: ASJA Press, 2007.

WEBSITES

The Cato Institute: cato.org

Center for a Stateless Society: c4ss.org

Foundation for Economic Education: fee.org

The Institute for Humane Studies: theihs.org

Libertarian Party: lp.org

Liberty magazine: libertyunbound.com

Ludwig Von Mises Institute: mises.org

The Nolan Chart: nolanchart.com

Reason Foundation: reason.org

Reason magazine: reason.com

ABOUT THE AUTHOR

TODD SEAVEY has written for such libertarian or libertarian-tolerating individuals and organizations as SpliceToday.com, John Stossel, Judge Andrew Napolitano, *Reason* magazine, *New York Press*, *New York Post*, *Wall Street Journal*, the American Council on Science and Health, *Skeptical Inquirer*, *National Review*, *Chronicles*, Spiked-Online.com, and TheFederalist.com.

He has also written comedy, Justice League comic books, and advertising and has appeared on *Style Court*, *The Run*, and CSPAN-2. He is a graduate and survivor of Brown University and lives in New York City, where he often organizes debates, speeches, and bar events. He can be found on Twitter, Facebook, and Blogger. His wonderful New England-dwelling parents taught him not to commit assault, theft, or fraud.

ABOUT THE ILLUSTRATOR

NATHAN SMITH (a.k.a. bluefluke) is a writer and illustrator who specializes in the classical western esoteric tradition. His notable works include "The Psychonaut Field Manual," "Am I Evil?", and the "Discordian Tarot Collection." See his art at *bluefluke.deviantart.com* or *bluefluke.tumblr.com*

THE FOR BEGINNERS® SERIES

AFRICAN HISTORY FOR BEGINNERS	ISBN 978-1-934389-18-8
ANARCHISM FOR BEGINNERS	ISBN 978-1-934389-32-4
ARABS & ISRAEL FOR BEGINNERS	ISBN 978-1-934389-16-4
ART THEORY FOR BEGINNERS	ISBN 978-1-934389-47-8
ASTRONOMY FOR BEGINNERS	ISBN 978-1-934389-25-6
AYN RAND FOR BEGINNERS	ISBN 978-1-934389-37-9
BARACK OBAMA FOR BEGINNERS, AN ESSENTIAL GUIDE	ISBN 978-1-934389-44-7
BEN FRANKLIN FOR BEGINNERS	ISBN 978-1-934389-48-5
BLACK HISTORY FOR BEGINNERS	ISBN 978-1-934389-19-5
THE BLACK HOLOCAUST FOR BEGINNERS	ISBN 978-1-934389-03-4
BLACK PANTHERS FOR BEGINNERS	ISBN 978-1-939994-39-4
BLACK WOMEN FOR BEGINNERS	ISBN 978-1-934389-20-1
BUDDHA FOR BEGINNERS	ISBN 978-1-939994-33-2
BUKOWSKI FOR BEGINNERS	ISBN 978-1-939994-37-0
CHOMSKY FOR BEGINNERS	ISBN 978-1-934389-17-1
CIVIL RIGHTS FOR BEGINNERS	ISBN 978-1-934389-89-8
CLIMATE CHANGE FOR BEGINNERS	ISBN 978-1-934389-27-0
DADA & SURREALISM FOR BEGINNERS	ISBN 978-1-934389-00-3
DANTE FOR BEGINNERS	ISBN 978-1-934389-67-6
DECONSTRUCTION FOR BEGINNERS	ISBN 978-1-934389-26-3
DEMOCRACY FOR BEGINNERS	ISBN 978-1-934389-36-2
DERRIDA FOR BEGINNERS	ISBN 978-1-934389-11-9
EASTERN PHILOSOPHY FOR BEGINNERS	ISBN 978-1-934389-07-2
EXISTENTIALISM FOR BEGINNERS	ISBN 978-1-934389-21-8
FANON FOR BEGINNERS	ISBN 978-1-934389-87-4
FDR AND THE NEW DEAL FOR BEGINNERS	ISBN 978-1-934389-50-8
FOUCAULT FOR BEGINNERS	ISBN 978-1-934389-12-6
FRENCH REVOLUTIONS FOR BEGINNERS	ISBN 978-1-934389-91-1
GENDER & SEXUALITY FOR BEGINNERS	ISBN 978-1-934389-69-0
GREEK MYTHOLOGY FOR BEGINNERS	ISBN 978-1-934389-83-6
HEIDEGGER FOR BEGINNERS	ISBN 978-1-934389-13-3
THE HISTORY OF CLASSICAL MUSIC FOR BEGINNERS	ISBN 978-1-939994-26-4
THE HISTORY OF OPERA FOR BEGINNERS	ISBN 978-1-934389-79-9
ISLAM FOR BEGINNERS	ISBN 978-1-934389-01-0
JANE AUSTEN FOR BEGINNERS	ISBN 978-1-934389-61-4
JUNG FOR BEGINNERS	ISBN 978-1-934389-76-8
KIERKEGAARD FOR BEGINNERS	ISBN 978-1-934389-14-0
LACAN FOR BEGINNERS	ISBN 978-1-934389-39-3
LINCOLN FOR BEGINNERS	ISBN 978-1-934389-85-0
LINGUISTICS FOR BEGINNERS	ISBN 978-1-934389-28-7
MALCOLM X FOR BEGINNERS	ISBN 978-1-934389-04-1
MARX'S DAS KAPITAL FOR BEGINNERS	ISBN 978-1-934389-59-1
MCLUHAN FOR BEGINNERS	ISBN 978-1-934389-75-1
MUSIC THEORY FOR BEGINNERS	ISBN 978-1-939994-46-2
NIETZSCHE FOR BEGINNERS	ISBN 978-1-934389-05-8
PAUL ROBESON FOR BEGINNERS	ISBN 978-1-934389-81-2
PHILOSOPHY FOR BEGINNERS	ISBN 978-1-934389-02-7
PLATO FOR BEGINNERS	ISBN 978-1-934389-08-9
POETRY FOR BEGINNERS	ISBN 978-1-934389-46-1
POSTMODERNISM FOR BEGINNERS	ISBN 978-1-934389-09-6
RELATIVITY & QUANTUM PHYSICS FOR BEGINNERS	ISBN 978-1-934389-42-3
SARTRE FOR BEGINNERS	ISBN 978-1-934389-15-7
SAUSSURE FOR BEGINNERS	ISBN 978-1-939994-41-7
SHAKESPEARE FOR BEGINNERS	ISBN 978-1-934389-29-4
STANISLAVSKI FOR BEGINNERS	ISBN 978-1-939994-35-6
STRUCTURALISM & POSTSTRUCTURALISM FOR BEGINNERS	ISBN 978-1-934389-10-2
WOMEN'S HISTORY FOR BEGINNERS	ISBN 978-1-934389-60-7
UNIONS FOR BEGINNERS	ISBN 978-1-934389-77-5
U.S. CONSTITUTION FOR BEGINNERS	ISBN 978-1-934389-62-1
ZEN FOR BEGINNERS	ISBN 978-1-934389-06-5
ZINN FOR BEGINNERS	ISBN 978-1-934389-40-9

WWW.FORBEGINNERSBOOKS.COM